T*he* ROSSACHS
History & Guide

The TROSSACHS
History & Guide

William F. Hendrie

TEMPUS

As Headmaster of Lothian School Camps from 1971 to 1995, I dedicate this book to Bob and Anne Ralston and family, to my predecessor as headmaster, Guthrie Pollock, and to all the members of staff at Dounans Residential Outdoor Education Centre, Aberfoyle, who helped ensure that the thousands of pupils who stayed there discovered the treasures of the Trossachs.

First published 2004

Tempus Publishing Ltd
The Mill, Brimscombe Port
Stroud, Gloucestershire GL5 2QG
www.tempus-publishing.com

British Library Cataloguing in Publication Data.
A catalogue record for this book is available from the British Library.

ISBN 0 7524 2991 4

Typesetting and origination by Tempus Publishing.
Printed in Great Britain.

Contents

Acknowledgements

My thanks to Forest Enterprise, Scottish Centres, Scottish Wool Centre, West of Scotland Water and Eric Brown, Harry Dott, Captain John Fraser, John Hair, Captain John Howells, Ian Nicholson, Guthrie Pollock, Bob Ralston, Anne Ralston, Raymond Thomson, Fergus Wood and all of the other people and organisations who so kindly answered my questions and provided me with information. I am grateful also to Eric Simpson for computer advice and to my publisher Campbell McCutcheon for his assistance with the production of this book.

My special thanks to Dr Arthur Down, who accompanied me on many of my travels and took many of the photographs which illustrate this book, and to the others who have provided additional pictures.

William F. Hendrie
Torphichen

Introduction

The Trossachs was the name given originally to the narrow gorge between Loch Achray and Loch Katrine. Now, however, the term is applied to the whole of the rugged miniature Highlands, whose sparkling lochs and heather and bracken-clad hills attract many visitors to the magnificently scenic area surrounding Callander and Aberfoyle, which very appropriately forms part of Scotland's first National Park. Adding greatly to the appeal of this compact area is the distinct contrast between the Highlands and the Lowlands, which can be appreciated here more dramatically than anywhere else in Scotland as a result of the Highland Boundary Fault Line, which very visibly divides these lands.

Trossachs means stony or bristly land, and, as this description suggests, it was originally a rough, wild and sometimes dangerous area of Scotland. This remoteness continued until the middle of the nineteenth century, when improvements in transport coincided with the great interest in Scotland created by the royal visits made by Queen Victoria and Prince Albert. While the royal couple travelled farther north and chose the banks of the river Dee as the site for their Scottish royal holiday hideaway at Balmoral, the Trossachs was much more accessible to the early tourists who followed their royal example and invaded Scotland in ever-increasing numbers.

These pioneering nineteenth-century sightseers were also encouraged to include the Trossachs in their itineraries by the great-grandfather of Scottish tourism, Sir Walter Scott. His most famous poem, although entitled 'The Lady of the Lake', was so clearly based on Loch Katrine that his readers had no difficulty picking out landmarks and beauty spots in the same way that modern television viewers enjoy identifying scenes from popular modern drama series such as *Monarch of the Glen*. Sir Walter's novels were the blockbusters of his time and none more so than his famous adventure yarn *Rob Roy*, which featured incidents set throughout the Trossachs, from the outlaw's birth place at Glengyle on the western shores of Loch Katrine to the famous 'Affray at the Clachan of Aberfoyle'.

The Trossachs contains the United Kingdom's largest forest, the Queen Elizabeth Forest Park, and, as well as sightseeing, this wooded area offers visitors opportunities for outdoor pursuits ranging from pony trekking, a pursuit which originated there in the years after the Second World War, to the latest way to leave the beaten track by taking part in the exciting sport of all-terrain biking. The stories and legends which make the Trossachs such a romantic area range from the Revd Robert Kirk's encounters with the fairies, fawns, elves and other wee folk around Aberfoyle, to how Loch Katrine acquired its name from a beautiful virgin maiden.

The Trossachs has sometimes been described as Glasgow's playground, but increasingly its appeal is being appreciated by visitors from much further afield than Scotland's largest city, which is situated only 30 miles to the south. The chapters which follow aim to inform readers so that they can gain the most from their visit to this small but scenically superlative territory of soaring mountains, shimmering lochs and solitary glens.

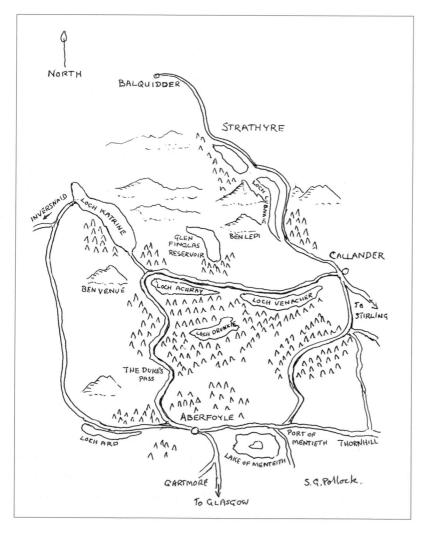

Map of the Trossachs. Original drawing by Guthrie Pollack.

chapter one

The Capital of the Trossachs

'Definitely the best place in Scotland to make a date!' This and dozens of other similar cryptic clues in countless charity quizzes over the years have made the name of Callander one of the best known amongst Scotland's inland holiday resorts.

Callander, however, should not be written off as simply the answer to a quiz question. Conveniently situated only a drive north on the A81 road from Scotland's largest centre of population, Glasgow, Callander is the acknowledged capital of the Trossachs. Callander has for decades also provided the perfect answer for families looking for somewhere 'nice' to visit on day outings. Long before the development of theme parks and other modern commercial attractions, which tempt families to spend not just their time but their money, Callander was already synonymous with somewhere special for summer holiday treats and this has indeed been its attraction for over a century and a half.

While now a peaceful holiday destination, Callander owes its origins to one of the most warlike periods in Scottish history, the time of the Jacobites and the rebellion or uprising led by Prince Charles Edward Stewart, otherwise known as Bonnie Prince Charlie. For the lands on which Callander now stands once belonged to the Drummond family who supported the Young Pretender, or Claimant to the Throne, as Charles was often described. However their loyalty to the prince cost the family dear as, following the crushing defeat of his Jacobite cause at the Battle of Culloden near Inverness in 1746, the government established the Commissioners for Forfeited Estates. The Commissioners decreed that the Drummonds and all other Jacobite supporters must be punished severely through the confiscation of their lands. At the same time the government was also determined to tame the wild Highlands once and for all. It was decided that the best way of achieving this would be by opening up the whole area through the construction of roads, which would allow military patrols easier and safer access. A second scheme was the establishment of planned towns along the routes of these new roads. There it was hoped the clansmen could be settled and an ever-watchful eye kept upon them.

On the road north from Stirling to Crianlarich, it was decided that a site on the banks of the river Teith would be ideal for one of these developments and thus Callander was established at a point where, according to a plan drawn a few years earlier in 1739, only a handful of crofts had previously straggled the roadside.

Callander thus became one of Scotland's first planned towns. With mathematical precision it was decreed that the streets should be 60ft wide and that the feus bordering them should be 60ft deep. From the outset the roads followed a pattern similar to that which exists today, with what is now long, straight Main Street transected by three shorter roads running from east to west. Only the names have changed. What was first known as Kirk Street became Cross Street and Bridge Street, while the so-called Street to the Bridge, which did not at the time exist as the river Teith for many years had to be crossed by ferry, became the present North and South Church Streets. On the original plans there was a Square Street and provision for a small marketplace, where the much larger Ancaster Square now provides the town with its lively heart.

Such a well laid out plan would no doubt have appealed to some of Callander's earliest visitors, the Romans, and the famous 'Lost Legend' is believed to have marched this way as it trekked north beyond Antonine's Wall, the outermost limit of their nation's vast empire, in a bid to safeguard it from the troublesome Picts. While little is accurately known about this dangerous Roman advance into the Highlands, it is believed that before they were overcome the legionaries built a camp at Callander with lookout towers over the river Teith and there are various earthworks around the town which may have Roman origins, but are more probably glacial remains.

While the area where Callander is now situated therefore had links with the south throughout history, and much improved ones provided by the government to help suppress the clansmen after the Jacobite Rebellion of 1745, it was not until a century later, in the 1850s, that it became easy to reach with the construction of a railway line from Stirling. Built by the Dunblane, Doune & Callander Railway, the route of the embankments along which the track was laid can still be seen on the southern approaches to the town. The company's first railway station was at the south end of the town and, as this was as far as the line originally ran, Callander initially became the railhead for the whole of the surrounding district.

Soon after the coming of the first steam trains to the town in 1858, a Victorian guidebook described Callander as 'an especially convenient centre for visitors who wish to explore this scenically spectacular area of Scotland'. The guidebook continues:

> The little town is charmingly situated on the banks of the river Teith, in the sheltering lea of the handsome 2,875ft-high Ben Ledi, whose slopes rise two and a half miles to the north-west. Callander is also an incomparable rendezvous for anglers. A first

Callander's many tourist shops welcome hundreds of thousands of visitors every year. This view looks north along the east side of Main Street. (Arthur Down)

class return train ticket from Stirling to Callander may be obtained for four shillings, while the third class fare for the same journey is only one shilling and ten pence.

Shortly after reaching Callander, the Dunblane, Doune & Callander Railway was taken over by the Scottish Central Railway. With the rapid spread of rail travel throughout Scotland, mergers between the original small companies which brought this means of mass transport to individual towns soon became common and in 1865 the Scottish Central was in turn swallowed by the famous Scottish Caledonian, with expansionist plans to extend the Callander line all the way north and west to Oban, although it took until 1880 to reach there.

As the new track progressed through the town, it made sense to relocate Callander Station. The site of this second station, where Victorian travellers subsequently alighted to enjoy the delights which nineteenth-century Callander had to offer, can still be seen in the bus and car park. It is situated in what is still known as Station Road, to the right at the north end of Main Street, although the line has been closed since October 1965. Adjacent to where the old station was sited still stands the impressive turreted, three-storey Dreadnought Hotel, built originally to welcome nineteenth-century travellers.

The Dreadnought pre-dates the coming of the railway, having first opened as a modest inn in 1802. Ever since, many guests have been puzzled by its unusual name and modern visitors often ponder whether there is a connection between the name of the hotel in this inland Scottish town and the mighty First World War battleships known as Dreadnoughts. There is none. Callander's Dreadnought does however derive its title from an equally warlike source: a clan battle cry.

11

From the seventeenth century onwards, the large and important feu on the corner of Callander's Main Street, which the hotel occupies, belonged to the Clan McNab and 'Dreadnought' was their proud motto.

When the railway reached Callander, the Dreadnought was one of several large establishments which developed to serve the needs of the new train excursionists. With its two large silver-painted stone lions guarding either side of the entrance, it still retains the feel of a grand hotel, an atmosphere carefully maintained by its owners British Trust Hotels (BTH). BTH has been in the catering and hospitality trade for over a century and this has satisfactorily ensured that the Dreadnought, while retaining many of its Victorian features, has also kept up to date with modern expectations and so has survived much longer than some of the town's other hotels.

One hotel which was long ago demolished was the Callander Hydropathic Establishment, whose site is now occupied by the caravan park to the northwest of the town. Opening in 1882 the Callander Hydro was built on the same impressive scale as those spa resort hotels which still flourish at Crieff, Peebles and Pitlochry, and its water cures and expensive health treatments soon became popular with many wealthy guests. As well as spending their holiday enjoying costly medical fads and fancies, it was also *de rigueur* for this newly rich leisure class to copy Queen Victoria and Prince Albert by venturing to explore the rugged grandeur of this wild country in which they had come to stay. Thus from the Hydro, as from Callander's array of other hotels which flourished in the town during these decades, horse-drawn wagonettes set out daily to transport guests to the beauty spots of the Trossachs.

Another hotel which has disappeared is The Palace. It is described in the Victorian guidebook as 'the truly palatial Palace, whose gleaming white walls stand out from the tall green trees, which surround its private grounds, where guests may enjoy leisurely strolls amongst its colourfully planted gardens and carefully trimmed green lawns'.

Some of Callander's smartest Victorian visitors were the families of rich Glasgow businessmen, who came to the little Perthshire town for the whole of the summer season, choosing not to stay in any of the hotels, but to rent one of the fine new villas which local builders W. & T. Adams had enterprisingly built on the western outskirts on the Leny Estate, on what became known as the Leny Feus, a visit to which still makes a pleasant walk to the north of the town.

Preparation for the coming of these rich city folk was a major operation in Callander, because while they brought with them their principal servants such as butler, cook and nanny, they also employed additional local staff. Amongst them were many of the town's schoolchildren, and teachers complained about girls and boys playing truant in preparation for the Glasgow families' arrival, the girls to earn pocket money by cleaning the houses and the boys to cash in on tidying the large gardens. On the day of their arrival the incomers hired a fleet of horse-drawn vehicles to take them out to their rented homes at the west end of the town and quickly settled into their holiday routine. After the first week, however, the fathers had to return to work in their Glasgow offices and travelled

This historic Caledonian Railway poster, *c.*1910, advertises a Pullman observation car excursion to Oban and back via Callander. The line through Callander was one of the most scenically beautiful in Scotland but closed in the 1960s after a rock fall and landslide. (Peter Croxford)

The Caledonian Railway which served Callander advertised itself as 'The True Line', but sometimes alterations to timetables were required as this poster for the month of December 1912 shows. Amongst the trains listed were the express ones from Callander to Glasgow, which allowed city businessmen to holiday with their families in the villas at the Leny Feus or at hotels in the town yet be at their desks on time each weekday morning. (Peter Croxford)

Left Stone lions guard the main entrance to the Dreadnought Hotel, whose tubs of flowers and hanging floral baskets add a splash of colour to the Callander scene. (Arthur Down)

Right The turreted three-storey high premises of Callander's well-known Dreadnought Hotel dominate the scene at the northern end of Main Street. The hotel, which first opened for business in 1802 and was greatly expanded to cater for the growth in tourism after the coming of the railway in the middle of the century, takes its unusual name from the war cry of the Clan McNab on whose land it stands. The Clan McNab motto is 'Let all fear be absent' and its crest is the head of a savage, with the prickly bramble as its clan plant. Septs of the Clan McNab include those with the surnames of Abbott, Cleland, Dewar, Gilfillan, Gillan, MacLellan and MacNair. Those with the family name of Callander are linked to the MacFarlanes, whose clan territory was originally Loch Lomondside. (Arthur Down)

every morning to Callander Station, from where a fast train conveyed them to their desks in time for nine o'clock. In the evening the express transported them back to Callander where, in the Square in front of the Dreadnought, horse-drawn carriages waited to transport them back to their holiday homes at Leny Feus in time for dinner.

From the very beginning Callander learned how to cater for its visitors and so it continues to do to the present day, whether they wish to picnic in the park known as the Meadows which stretches out along the grassy banks of the Teith, or to enjoy Scottish high tea in one of the restaurants in Main Street.

For the uninitiated, five or six o'clock high tea in Scotland is a more substantial meal than the dainty afternoon tea of cucumber or egg and cress sandwiches served an hour earlier in England, as it always includes a main course such as fried haddock and chips, hot steak pie or cold salmon mayonnaise and salad. The main course is served with toasted bread and pots of tea and is followed by a choice of what are known as 'tea breads', such as pink-iced or cream-filled cookies and pancakes, as the daintily delectable drop scones are known. Next comes that Scottish classic, shortbread, made perhaps locally by Callander's oldest baker's shop, Donald Campbell's, in North Ancaster Square. They have been baking shortbread to a traditional recipe ever since they first opened for business in the town in 1830. Then finally comes the *pièce de résistance* of every Scottish high tea, a selection of cream cakes presented on a tiered, glass-shelved, silver cake stand. High tea, although served an hour or two earlier, is thus a very filling substitute for dinner and its great glory is, of course, that it still leaves time to develop an appetite again before bedtime, for supper to round off the evening very satisfactorily at nine or ten o'clock at night.

Ever since the relaxation of petrol restrictions after the Second World War, Callander has catered well for those who seek such suppers, as it became the number one destination for so-called 'evening mystery bus tours'. On these

Above Callander Meadows along the shores of the Teith are a popular summer picnic spot, but in winter the river often floods its banks. Behind rises Callander Craigs, where there are many pleasant walks. (Arthur Down)

Left A fine arched stone bridge now carries the road to Glasgow and the south across the Teith, but during Callander's early years the river had to be crossed by ferry. (Arthur Down)

short excursions it was the rule that passengers were never told the destination, but they were usually delighted if it turned out to be Callander, because all of the restaurants, tearooms, ice cream shops and cafés along the length of Main Street stayed open late, before this was common practice in most other Scottish towns. To this day the tradition persists and Callander is still the last stop before returning home for many day trippers.

Of an evening it is possible to eat one's way from one end of Callander to the other. Start by popping into Johnson's famous fudge shop for a taste of tablet, a sort of soft, sugary mouth-wateringly delicious toffee. Tablet was the favourite

The black and white mock-Tudor frontage of Bridgend House Hotel is a well-known Callander landmark. (Arthur Down)

'sweetie' of Scottish author J.J. Bell's hero Wee Macgreegor, who has become Scotland's equivalent of England's William Brown of *Just William* fame and America's Tom Sawyer.

Next move on along Main Street to sample the delights of the town's fish and chip shops and ice cream parlours. In the window of one of these ice cream parlours – the Ben Ledi café which celebrated its centenary in 2004 – is the animated figure of a wee school laddie who has licked his way through several generations of cones and wafers, thus giving rise to the oft-quoted expression 'often licked but never beaten'. Every year at the end of October, as Halloween approaches, the wee fellow even swaps his school uniform to keep up the old Scottish tradition of going 'guising' by dressing up in a costume consisting of a witch's outfit complete with black cape, conical hat and broomstick. Callander definitely does not miss any tricks in its efforts to keep its visitors entertained and happy.

It would be totally incorrect, however, to picture Callander as simply cheap and cheerful. As an inland holiday resort all tastes and requirements are catered for, and for those who seek *haute cuisine* it has for decades been available in the genteel country house setting of the Roman Camp Hotel. Discreetly hidden from view at the southern end of Main Street, to reach it go through the stone-arched entrance on the south side of the road and walk to the end of the long, narrow hedge-lined drive. Roman Camp takes its name from the Roman encampment which local tradition maintains existed nearby on the shores of the river Teith. The picturesque house, with its unusual pink-harled, rough-cast walls beneath its steeply sloping grey-slate roof, resembles a French château, with its witch's hat, pepper-pot-like topped turrets and immaculately clipped green hedges, lined like sentinels on either side of its porticoed main entrance.

Carved deep into the stonework above the old wooden front door to Roman Camp is the motto 'Gang Warily', but it is a warning which seems unnecessary, for once inside the house the atmosphere is more that of a warm-welcoming country cottage than of a stern, cold Highland castle. Moving on from the wood-lined reception hall to explore further it is interesting historically to find that parts of the long, low, rambling building date all the way back to the seventeenth century.

It was as long ago as 1625, during the reign of King James VI of Scotland and I of England, that this sheltered setting on the banks of the Teith was chosen by the Duke of Perth as the site for his country hunting lodge, with excellent brown trout fishing available on the stretch of river flowing through its grounds, and herds of red deer roaming the neighbouring hills. The fishing is still available free of charge to hotel guests.

To this day Roman Camp still produces many of the ingredients for the meals which it serves, because although listed as being of particular historic impor-tance, its walled garden is still fully cultivated. Although very much a working garden, guests are welcome to push open the tall wrought-iron gate to explore. Once behind the high, sheltering sandstone walls, it has very much the feel of a secret garden. It is, however, no secret that the garden supplies many of the fresh herbs and varied vegetables which the chefs in the kitchen turn into the inventive dishes for which Roman Camp is famed. The garden's multitude of flowers also add to the decor of the dining room as well as to the sitting room, library and other parts of the interior.

Throughout Roman Camp are many features of architectural interest, ranging from the linenfold wood panelling of its ancient walls to the ornate plasterwork of its ceilings. Most famous of all its historic curiosities is the tiny secret chapel carefully concealed in a nook, a little corner tucked away behind one of the walls. This is a sad reminder of the days of religious intolerance in Scotland's past when members of the Church of Rome had to worship in secret for fear of persecution. Now such intolerance is in direct contrast to the friendly welcome which Roman Camp's current hosts extend to their guests, no matter what their creed or colour.

In the eighteenth century Roman Camp became the home of Reginald, Viscount of Esher, who was personal equerry to King George III. It soon became the Esher family's favourite country retreat and to show their appreciation for the town Viscount Esher gifted Callander a decorative little water fountain.

After centuries as a gracious private residence, it was not until 1939 that Roman Camp opened its doors to the public for the first time as a country house hotel; present-day guests can still see the Esher family's ornate armorial bearings with their gold Lion Rampant on a scarlet background on their coat of arms preserved in stained glass in the window of the library. With its crowded shelves the library is a particular temptation to browsers and, once a book has been selected, there are deep-armed easy chairs in which to settle back and enjoy a good read. Roman Camp is truly a place for all seasons and on cooler days the

Roman Camp Country House Hotel lies tucked away at the end of a long driveway at the southern end of the town. Its name is a reminder that Roman legionaries reached Callander on their advance beyond Antonine's Wall into the hostile Highlands of Scotland and established an outpost in this area. (Arthur Down)

library has a real log fire kept aglow with timber gathered from along the woodland path which winds through the 20 acres of secluded grounds.

Around Callander there are also many popular public walks. At the Roman Camp end of town, on the opposite side of the main road, one of the most famous walks since Victorian times has been the gentle 2-mile climb up to the spectacular Falls of Bracklinn. The route is clearly signposted past the town's eighteen-hole golf course and the site of the original railway terminal, before the later line was extended further north and the station adjacent to the Dreadnought Hotel was constructed.

It was around this part of the town that veteran soldiers, returning in 1763 from what has since become known as the Seven Years' War against the French, were rewarded with plots of land on which to establish crofts and keep themselves and their families by growing their own food. The land which they cultivated is now covered by one of the fairways of the golf course. As the path continues to climb, there are impressive views to the south out over the whole of the town, until the falls themselves provide a fitting climax to the expedition. The falls are formed by the rushing, roaring waters of the river Keltie. Try to visit the waterfalls after a really heavy downpour of rain, because when in full spate this Highland burn turns itself into a truly terrifying torrent as it first throws itself over a succession of what geologists describe as 'mature cataracts' before finally flinging itself a good 50ft down through a rocky gorge to the deep, dark pool below. As it does so the thunderous noise is deafening and spray and foam fill the air, providing a fitting reminder of the line in 'The Lady of the Lake' where Sir Walter Scott, referring to his hero, writes: 'I grant him brave but wild as Bracklinn's thundering wave'.

Much more peaceful is Callander's other celebrated walk to the top of the 2,875ft-high Ben Ledi. This is a longer trek as the distance from the centre of the town to the summit is about 4½ miles and in places it is a steep climb. Ben Ledi is derived from the Gaelic words Beinn, which means a hill or mountain, and Leda, meaning gods, and according to tradition the summit of this Mountain of the Gods was a sacred site for the ancient Druids. This was especially so late each spring at the beginning of May, when the ancient pagan fire ceremonies of Beltane were celebrated on its summit, on either the first or third day of the month.

The exact nature of these superstitious rituals conducted at the summit of Ben Ledi was a closely guarded secret, just as the Druid acts of worship conducted at Stonehenge are to this day, but as the first rays of dawn lit its peak, they always culminated in the lighting of a huge bonfire to welcome the warmth of summer and to symbolise the long, light nights which were to follow. While no part of Scotland enjoys a visit from the midnight sun, the long 'White Nights' of May and June, when it is possible to play golf until ten o'clock or later and when midnight is a deep blue and it is never truly dark, are such an attractive feature of our northern summers that it is equally a modern mystery why the tourist authority (www.visitScotland.com) does not make more of them in its publicity as these lingering light nights extend hours for sightseeing on May and June evenings.

One local person who has already capitalised upon Ben Ledi's superstitious past is Stirling author Rennie McOwan, whose children's novel *When the Mountain Moved* cleverly weaves the legends into its intriguing plot.

Adding still further to Ben Ledi's mysteries is the legend of how the little loch near the summit, Lochan-nan-corp, meaning the small lake of dead bodies, took its name. According to the legend, one winter, while accompanying a coffin on its slow way from Glen Finglas, to the west of Callander near Brig O'Turk, to the kirkyard to the north of the Pass of Leny for burial, a funeral party was attempting to take a shortcut across Lochan-nan-corp's frozen surface when the ice began to groan and moan. Suddenly, with a crack described as loud enough to awaken the soul of the deceased in the coffin, the ice gave way and all those accompanying it were plunged into the dark, icy waters. Desperately they tried to struggle to the shore, but one by one were overcome by the numbing cold and drowned in the depths of Lochan-nan-corp.

Despite its eerie legends, however, the views from Ben Ledi's summit are certainly fit for the gods after whom it was named. On a clear day the panorama stretches from the outline of the Bass Rock looming out of the waters of the Firth of Forth, 2 miles off North Berwick in the east, to the Paps or Breasts of Jura to the north-west, on the opposite (west) coast of Scotland.

More about ancient superstitions and the legends of the area, from saints to sinners and from giants to wee folk, can be discovered at Breadalbane Folklore Centre. The centre is housed in the old stone-built watermill which stands beside the Falls of Dochart at the entrance to the village of Killin, where audio-visual and film animation techniques bring local tales to life. Nearby is the spot beside the waterfalls, featured on many Scottish pictorial calendars, where the

The soaring stone spire of St Kessog's kirk, now the Rob Roy Centre and Callander Tourist Information Office, became known to millions of television viewers when it featured in the opening shots of the original series of *Dr Finlay's Casebook*. In the foreground is the tall lion rampant-crowned column of the town's war memorial in Ancaster Square. (Arthur Down)

mystical St Fillian, the Irish Prince, Celtic priest and Christian missionary, is said to have sat and contemplated. St Fillian is credited with performing many miracles and King Robert the Bruce claimed he inspired him to victory at Bannockburn in 1314.

Inside the Folklore Centre the stones from the nearby river, which St Fillian blessed centuries ago, can be seen. It is believed that different stones heal different parts of the body. The prophecies of the Lady of Lawers and other legends of Breadalbane are also illustrated, and the centre tells the histories of four clans with links to the area: the Campbells, MacGregors, MacLarens and McNabs. The restored waterwheel can also be inspected.

Callander also has a visitor interpretation centre in Main Street in the fine stone-built St Kessog's kirk, with its slender lofty spire overlooking the town's

Ancaster Square. Built in 1889, St Kessog's took its name from the Irish follower of St Columba who is reputed to have brought Christianity to the area and after whom the strange-shaped mound overlooking the river Teith is also named, near whose base the town's earliest place of worship was originally situated. No trace of this survives, but nearby is the town's early burial ground with its watchtower built to protect the graves from danger of attack by the early nineteenth-century resurrectionists, or body snatchers as they were more commonly known, as they plied their grisly trade to supply specimens to the anatomy departments of the medical schools at both Edinburgh and Glasgow Universities. Now the centre, which has occupied the Victorian premises of the former kirk since its congregation moved to join the worshippers at Callander parish church in South Church Street, is dedicated to the life and legends of Scotland's answer to England's Robin Hood, the flaming red-haired Rob Roy MacGregor. The Rob Roy Centre has enjoyed a great increase in visitors since the release of the Hollywood film about this local hero, with Irish actor Liam Neeson in the title role. In the centre's audio-visual theatre outlawed Rob talks to a fellow clansman and his controversial turbulent life is revealed in a series of flashbacks.

The centre also features entertainments ranging from folk singing and ceilidhs to illustrated talks about the history and natural wildlife of the area. During the summer, feature films are also shown. Most have a Scottish setting, from modern epics such as *Brave Heart*, starring Mel Gibson as Sir William Wallace, to vintage black and white favourites including Sir Compton MacKenzie's *Whisky Galore*, to the drama of the Clydeside shipbuilding yards in *Floodtide*, starring Rhona Anderson and Gordon Jackson, whom she later married.

As well as displays on the local wildlife of the area, the centre contains a life-size recreation of a Highland croft in which visitors can try using various implements, from stirring the contents of the porridge pot with a wooden hand-carved spirtle, to sweeping the large open hearth beside the fire with a besom broom. Set in such a fine former kirk, it is a pity the visitor centre does not also relate a bit about Callander's church history, because there are certainly amusing tales to tell. One such concerns the Revd James Robertson, a Victorian preacher who complained bitterly about the draught whistling through the front door and straight into the pulpit. The elders in the Kirk Session gave permission for the installation of a wooden screen, but at a subsequent meeting the cold minister complained yet again that it was 'made of timber, so green, that the opening will almost let in my little finger, not withstanding it being dabb'd with poty, over and above!' Hopefully he had better fortune in 1784, when he petitioned for a new gown, declaring that the his old one was showing 'the strongest features of old age'.

Callander has a modern community leisure centre with a 20m-long heated indoor swimming pool, jacuzzi, sauna, steam room, sunbeds, full-sized games hall, squash courts, indoor carpet bowls hall, state-of-the-art fitness suite, a floodlit all-weather tennis and basketball court and, particularly appropriate for its setting so close to the hills and nearby mountains, a challenging climbing wall on which to learn and practise the techniques of rock climbing. Other facilities include a crèche, meeting rooms, caféteria and bar. The leisure complex is situated on the southern outskirts of the town in Glasgow Road and is attached to the town's well-known secondary school, McLaren High.

McLaren High School takes its name from Callander's greatest benefactor, Donald McLaren. A rich and prosperous local farmer and merchant with his own fleet of horse-drawn carts to take his crops to market, he ensured that his vehicles never returned empty, but always brought back loads of goods which he could sell in the town to the local folk, thus earning further profits. He was always known as 'The Banker', as he provided the people of Callander and farmers in the surrounding area with their first banking facilities. While he used his profits to enjoy a lifestyle as befitted a successful man, indulging his hobby of breeding Highland cattle for his Corrycrone herd, named after his farm, he also, in true Scottish Presbyterian style, never forgot the needs of his fellow townsfolk.

At the time of the Disruption of the Church of Scotland in 1843, when many ministers left their churches over the question of whether congregations or the local establishment figures had the right to appoint them, McLaren did not immediately join the new cause. However, after becoming frustrated by the slow pace of change in the established Church of Scotland, he became a follower of the new Free Church. His decision not only helped the new church to which he gave generous amounts of money, but also revolutionised education in Callander.

Schooling first came to the Trossachs area in the 1700s, thanks to the Society for the Propagation of Christian Education, which opened a school in Brig O'Turk, but its schools, like the parish school provided in Callander, were poorly run. Now followers of the new Free Church had chosen freedom of worship, they were equally determined that their children benefit from the best possible education and Donald McLaren paid most of the salary for a new dominie. In 1844, classes were held on weekdays in the pews of the church occupied by worshippers on the Sabbath, but soon funds provided by McLaren and his fellow elders allowed the building of a primary school which outrivalled the parish school.

Pupils from Callander who wished to go on to secondary education had, however, to travel all the way to Stirling High School. In 1892, after much debate in the town, the Free School expanded to become McLaren High and since then has served secondary school-age pupils from all parts of the Trossachs. Some of these areas were considered so remote and the winter weather so dangerous that until recently McLaren High was one of the few local authority schools in Scotland with boarding facilities. The school had two hostels in the town in the form of Victorian villas, one for boys and one for girls, and these accommodated pupils from outlying districts as far away as Inversnaid on the shores of Loch Lomond to the west and as far north as Crianlarich. Road and transport improvements and swifter methods of snow clearing during the winter months now permit most pupils to return home each evening, although this may involve a bus journey of an hour or more and an equally early start again the next morning.

At one time pupils also travelled every day to McLaren High by rail from Crianlarich, and former pupils of the school still tell of the tricks and escapades which they delighted in getting up to in the crowded third class compartments of the train. The train did not have a corridor linking the compartments and so the enterprising scholars invented their own code which they tapped out on the wooden partitions to pass messages en route and check answers to their home-work. Thankfully the railway journey usually gave time for homework to be completed, or at least copied, because if it had not been done before they arrived at their classes the children knew full well that they were liable to be disciplined with several searing, stinging strokes of the traditional Scottish school punishment strap. This instrument of chastisement was known as the tawse, a name derived from the process involved in the production of the lithe supple leather from which this thonged puss o' nine tails was specially manu-factured by a firm of saddlers in the Fife mining village of Lochgelly near Cowdenbeath. By coincidence, on length and weight it painfully resembled the long leather belts with which the windows of every railway carriage compart-ment used to be raised and lowered, and the McLaren High boys used to smack their own palms with these straps on the morning journey to lessons, boasting that this made it easier for them to suffer the discomfort of actual real strokes if subsequently chastised by their teachers in the classroom.

The fields adjacent to the spacious playground at McLaren High are always especially busy on the final weekend in July, when they are the attractive setting for what Callander claims to be the World Highland Games. One of the largest events in Scotland, this lasts from Saturday morning until the following Sunday afternoon. The programme includes traditional heavy events such as tossing the caber, which takes its name from the Gaelic word for a tree trunk, and puttin' the stane, which consists of hurling a boulder through the air. It is from this Scottish test of strength that the famous Samson's Putting Stane, which is a well-known feature of the Callander landscape, takes its name. Perched precariously on the edge of the most easterly of the hills above the Trossachs Trail which runs from Callander to Loch Venachar and Loch Achray, Samson's Stane is described by geologists as an erratic boulder, probably carried down from Glen Dochart by a glacier during the last great Scottish Ice Age. When temperatures rose and the glacier was unable to carry the stone as it retreated to the north-west, it was deposited precariously, where it still remains.

Returning to Callander on the A81, in Bridge Street notice the McLaren High School's fine original nineteenth-century stone-built building with its neat little curved, porticoed façade, now the premises of Callander primary school. The road then crosses the solidly built sandstone bridge over the river Teith, where originally a ferryboat plied. In summer the Teith looks calm and peaceful, but in winter it can change into a swollen torrent. In 1996 floodwater inundated many shops, cafés and other premises in Main Street, but all managed to re-open in time for the spring holidaymakers.

As one of Scotland's most successful tourist centres, Callander has many other attractions to offer. These include the Hamilton Toy Collection at 111 Main

Street, just to the south of Ancaster Square, which is open daily from April to October and at weekends throughout the winter. Ancaster Square itself is named after the Earls of Ancaster, who, as descendants of the Drummond family, owned land in the area and after whom the former large well-known hotel – The Ancaster Arms – whose Victorian premises can still be seen on the corner of Main Street, was also named. Once the most distinctly Scottish of Callander's other visitor attractions was its Heather Centre, 1 mile to the east of the town on the approach road from Stirling, but this has now expanded to become the Keltie Market Gardens and produces a range of Alpine plants, specialising in colourful violas, diascias and gentians, for wholesale distribution throughout Britain.

In high summer Callander's Ancaster Square is also colourfully decorated with hanging baskets of scarlet and pink geraniums and other brightly flowering pot plants. This is the time of year for the annual Trossachs Festival, when pipers, folk singers, traditional musicians and Highland dancers perform on the open-air stage to the passing crowds of local shoppers and holidaymakers from around the world.

chapter two

Weaving a Path to Bonny Strathyre and Balquhidder

The A81 road north from Callander passes many of the substantial stone-built Victorian villas which featured in the BBC television version of Scottish author A.J. Cronin's novel *Dr Finlay's Casebook*, when the town was chosen in the 1960s to represent the fictitious Tannochbrae. One local home is still called Arden House, in memory of where the legendary Dr Cameron held his surgery, looked after by his devoted housekeeper, the saintly Janet. The earliest episodes of this still well-remembered television series were filmed in black and white, and what was missed by these early programmes is clearly seen in the blaze of hues of the flowers in the well-kept gardens which line the road from the town out to what was once the separate village of Kilmahog. At Kilmahog the road into the heart of the Trossachs branches left from the main road to Strathyre and on to Crianlarich. The original stone-built, whitewashed toll house still stands at the junction, its bay window sticking out so that travellers had no excuse or opportunity to pass without paying their dues.

Nowadays it is Kilmahog's two large woollen outlets which take their toll on the purses of passing tourists. Kilmahog also houses a Clan Tartan Centre where visitors can trace their Scottish clan heritage. New tartans featured include the Rotary tartan, the Salvation Army tartan and the British Airways tartan, worn by the airline's pipe band. Even Scotland's 'other national drink', Barr's Irn Bru, has its own bright orange-coloured tartan.

Continuing north on the main road, the commercialism of Kilmahog is left behind and the halt at the Forestry Commission car park on the right-hand side brings visitors back to nature. The famous Falls of Leny are accessible from here but care is required crossing the main road and climbing the narrow, often muddy, tree-lined path which leads to them. When the river Leny is in spate, these falls are spectacular as millions of gallons of water rush and foam and froth, like a commercial for a well-known brand of washing powder. Above the falls, the Leny is truly a Highland torrent, a turbulent unruly youth of a stream, while immediately below it suddenly slows and matures into the river which is

Above The Trossachs Woollen Mill with Hamish the Highland Bull in the foreground.

Right Weaving was the original occupation of many of the people of Callander, as Kilmahog Woollen Mill still reminds visitors. (Arthur Down)

soon to marry with the river Venachar, to give birth further downstream to the river Teith.

From the car park there is also a thirty-minute way-marked walk through the forest. The route rises quickly above the Pass of Leny and there are fine views south towards Callander and the Menteith Hills. Nearer at hand the walk provides views of the ancient oak wood planted to provide bark for the production of tannin for the Scottish leather industry and for the production of wood to be converted by burning into charcoal for use in iron-making. Under some of the trees there are traces of the sites where the charcoal used to be made and of the bloomeries where iron was smelted.

Further on through the Pass of Leny, a second car park on the left offers sweeping views across Loch Lubnaig from which the Balvaig flows into the river Teith. This 4-mile-long stretch of water, which starts 3½ miles north-west of Callander, is often described as 'gloomy Loch Lubnaig', and Victorian writer Alexander Smith in one of his essays dubbed it 'the loch of rueful countenance'. On a sunny day, however, the views across its half-mile width to the wooded hillside beyond at the foot of Ben Ledi and the 2,685ft-high Ben Vane are stunningly beautiful.

On the west bank of Lubnaig, the track bed of the former Callander to Crianlarich and Oban railway line, which has been closed since a massive landslide in 1965, has been converted into a cycle track leading all the way to Strathyre with plans to extend it to Crianlarich. The existing Loch Lubnaig link is one of several long-distance off-road cycle routes in the Callendar area and there are several cycle hire businesses.

The cycle route past Loch Lubnaig is flat except where it climbs to make a short detour into the forest above. Before long it comes out of the trees and descends again to the old railway and loch level from which further north a spur to the left leads over a suspension bridge and into Strathyre. Strathyre means the sheltered valley and is the appropriate setting for the Forestry Commission's well-designed timber log chalets for rent and a well-kept caravan and camping site.

This is the Bonny Strathyre of the old Scottish song. Strath is the Gaelic for a broad valley, as is also found in Strathspey in the Highlands and nearer at hand within the Trossachs at Strathard near Aberfoyle, and the valley here is indeed

The Falls of Leny are one of Scotland's most spectacular waterfalls. Below the falls the river Leny merges with the river Venachar to form the Teith. (Joan Down)

both broad and beautiful. Dominating the scene is Ben Sheann, which means the Mountain of the Fairies. This V-shaped valley was not, however, created by any fairy magic but by the sheer power of the glacier which travelled through this area during the last Scottish Ice Age. There are two way-marked walks through the forest at Strathyre. One runs north for approximately 2 miles and provides a circular route which takes approximately two and a half hours to complete. The second walk starts from the same car park and information centre on the southern approach to the village. It begins by following the same route as the first across the river and into the forest but then swings south to provide access to the slopes of Beinn an t'Sidhein. Signposting stops at the edge of the forest, some of whose trees were planted in the 1930s and 1940s by Head Forester Alistair Cameron, who was skilled at matching each species of tree to the best soil for it to flourish.

In the valley the hamlet of Strathyre stretches along both sides of the main road at the foot of the glen. Traffic-calming measures have been introduced at either end of the village to try to make it safer and more pleasant to stop and enjoy the facilities which it has to offer. These include two traditional inns and, in marked contrast, a modern village store. Near the shop is a small stone memorial. It was erected in 1883 to the memory of Dugald Buchanan. Born at Ardoch, Strathyre, in 1716, he became a teacher and evangelist. The inscription states that he was 'a true poet and was considered mighty knowledgeable in the scriptures'. It then quotes from his works in both English and Gaelic. One critic wrote that Buchanan's work 'contained a dramatic presentation of the comic and moral upheaval of the Day of Judgement'. Buchanan's own Day of Judgement came in 1768 when he died at Kinloch Rannoch. From there his body was borne back to Strathyre and he lies buried at Little Leny, the traditional burial place of the Buchanans. Reached by an arched gateway and guarded by a small watch house, to deter the nineteenth-century body snatchers, it is also the burial place of members of the Buchanan family who were relatives of American President McKinley, who was assassinated in 1901.

Members of a cycling club speed past the Ben Sheann Hotel in the middle of Strathyre Main Street. (Arthur Down)

This statue of Rob Roy MacGregor, by the queen's sculptor in Scotland, Benno Schotz, stands on the grassy slopes above the Albert Hall in Stirling. It was donated to the town, often known as the gateway to the Trossachs, by one of the clansman's proud descendants, Mr MacGregor Dick of Kilmarnock, who had previously sought to have it erected in Edinburgh. The Scottish capital declined to provide a site, perhaps remembering that Rob had once been an outlaw. Stirling gladly accepted the gift, and although Mr Dick sadly died before it could be erected, his wife travelled to the town to perform the unveiling ceremony. Rob is seen wielding his sword and carrying a targe, a circular Scottish shield. (Arthur Down)

While Dugald Buchanan's grave lies largely forgotten and unvisited, that of Scotland's equivalent to Robin Hood, Rob Roy MacGregor, certainly does not. In recent years the ancient graveyard where he lies buried has become a regular place of pilgrimage not only for members of the Clan Gregor, but for film fans from all over the world who thrilled at the 1990s film version of his life. To find the famous Rob Roy's last resting place it is necessary to continue north to the hamlet of Kingshouses. There, branch to the left and drive through the under-pass, which leads to the side road to the Glen of Balquhidder.

Kingshouses takes its name from its long whitewashed inn, which was estab-lished through the co-operation of the government and the local laird (the Scottish word for lord) on the new government road or King's Highway as it was known, built after the Jacobite uprisings of the 1700s, to enable the easier movement of troops and thus the easier subjugation of the Highlands. There were several Kingshouses in different parts of the Highlands, usually built on the site of the work camps established to build the original roads. Nowadays many are identified only by the existence of place names, but Kingshouses in Strathyre and the similarly named establishment in Glencoe are still open for business as inns.

Once off the main road and through the nearby underpass, drive west. After 2 miles, high on the slope to the right, below the present Balquhidder church and the picturesque ruins of the earlier one, is situated the graveyard where Scotland's most famous outlaw lies buried.

Rob Roy MacGregor was born on the remote shores at the head of Loch Katrine in 1671. His middle name, Roy, is derived from the Gaelic for red and he was indeed a redhead, as were many of his clansfolk. His other physical distinction was the length of his arms in comparison with his body, an attribute captured in the famous statue of him wielding his sword, designed by the queen's sculptor in Scotland, Benno Schotz, which stands on the slope above the Albert Hall in Stirling. Despite his comparatively short stature, Rob's long arms were said to give him massive strength.

Rob Roy's great chronicler, Sir Walter Scott, described him as follows:

His stature was not of the tallest, but his person was uncommonly strong and compact. The greatest peculiarities of his frame were the breadth of his shoulders, and the great, and almost disproportionate length of his arms; so remarkable indeed, that it was said he could, without stopping, tie the garters of his Highland hose, which are placed two inches below the knee. His countenance was open, manly, stern at periods of danger but frank and cheerful in his hours of festivity. His hair was dark red, thick, frizzled, and curled short around the face. His fashion of dress showed, of course, the knees and upper part of the leg, which was described to me as resembling that of a Highland bull, hirsute, with red hair and evincing muscular strength similar to that animal. To these personal qualifications must be added a masterly use of the Highland sword, in which his length of arm gave him great advantage – and a perfect and intimate knowledge of all of the recesses of the wild country in which he harboured, and the character of the various individuals, whether friendly or hostile, with whom he might come into contact.

Rob was third son of Lieutenant-Colonel Donald MacGregor of Glengyle and his wife Margaret Campbell. The family was staunchly Protestant. While still a youth, MacGregor became famed for his skill with a broadsword and at the age of eighteen fought bravely under Viscount 'Bonnie' Dundee at the Battle of Killiecrankie in 1689. He continued his army career as a soldier in the Lennox Watch, an organisation which promised protection to the Scottish Lowland farmers from the Highlanders in return for payment. This became known as blackmail, a word possibly derived from the Gaelic for rent and the fact that payment was often made in kind in the form of a Highland cow, which in the past were mainly black in colour in contrast to the more familiar toffee brown colour nowadays. Another version of the derivation of the word is that Rob and his fellow 'constables', as they became known, collected their protection money in the form of oatmeal and that the farmers described this as 'black meal', which became corrupted into 'blackmail'. However, no matter what the origins of the term blackmail, it is clear that the young Rob Roy saw nothing wrong in collecting it from the southern farmers to whom he offered protection.

By the time, four years later in 1693, Rob married Mary Campbell from Corner on the shores of Loch Lomond, he was therefore a comparatively wealthy young man and she was very much a cultured Highland lady, rather than the aggressive Helen into whom Sir Walter Scott chose to transform her for the sake of his story. The following year, when the name MacGregor was once again proscribed, Roy proudly adopted her surname.

At around this same time, whether because of the proscription of his clan or for other reasons, Rob gave up being a constable and became a crofter with lands at Craigrostoun and at Inversnaid on the shores of Loch Lomond. Continuing to prosper, he rented grazing land in Perthshire on the Braes of Balquhidder and became a cattle dealer. In 1711 he was sufficiently well off to raise a loan of £1,000 from the Duke of Montrose to increase his herd of Highland cattle. His business success, however, was brought to a sudden end when his head drover, who was a MacDonald, ran off with the letters of credit. MacGregor was left to face the consequences. Desperate for money he turned to cattle rustling. When the Duke of Montrose discovered this he declared Rob Roy bankrupt. Rob was subsequently gazetted in the official *Edinburgh Evening Courant* as an embezzler. On 3 October 1712, on Montrose's instigation, the Lord Advocate issued a warrant for his arrest and every magistrate and army officer in Scotland was urged to seize him. When Rob failed to answer the summons, he was declared an outlaw and in his absence Mary and their young family were evicted from their home at Craigrostoun by Graham of Killearn, the Duke of Montrose's estate factor.

Although officially outlawed, Rob still had friends and one of them, the Earl of Breadalbane, who had no love for his sworn political enemy Montrose, allowed Rob to lease land on his estate at Auchinchisallen in Glen Dochart. Rob, however, was still prevented from following his career as a cattle dealer and so, to support his wife and family, he was obliged to turn again to cattle and sheep rustling. He made many raids into the Lowlands and returned with his prizes to hide the cows and sheep in the traditional MacGregor fastnesses around Loch Katrine. Although highly successful as an outlaw, Rob Roy is always said to have bitterly resented the persecution for which he blamed the government, which, following the Union of the Parliaments in 1707, now met in distant London.

Thus alienated from the Protestant government cause, when the Old Pretender to the British throne, the Catholic James Edward Stewart, returned to Scotland in 1715 to raise the standard for the Jacobites, Rob supported the uprising and led the Clan MacGregor to fight for the rebel cause. He and his clansmen had several successes capturing the boats belonging to the Colquhons on Loch Lomond and seizing twenty-two government guns near Callander. At the final indecisive Battle of Sheriffmuir, which none the less ended the 1715 Jacobite attempt to recover the throne, Rob, however, played no part. Despite this he was thereafter accused of high treason. As a result, government redcoat soldiers marched to Auchinchisallen and pulled the thatch off MacGregor's home before burning it to the ground.

The following year in 1716, the Duke of Argyll, who like Rob Roy's wife Mary was a Campbell and indeed Chief of the Clan, tried to help the couple by giving them permission to build a new home on his estate at Glen Shira. Rob seized the opportunity for a new beginning, but Mary declined to follow him there and remained living on the shores of Loch Katrine.

During these troubled years, Rob was captured by the government troops on several occasions, but always managed to escape. Most famous was the occasion when he was caught to the west of Stirling. He was mounted on a horse and tied behind one of his captors to make the short journey to Stirling Castle. Rob, however, never reached the castle stronghold, because as they rode across the river Forth at the Fords of Frew, he succeeded in cutting through the leather belt which bound him and swam to his freedom. On another occasion Rob was imprisoned in the notorious Newgate Prison in London and sentenced to be punished by being transported to the colonies, but just as he was about to board the ship which was to take him into exile, he was pardoned by the king and was greeted as a hero upon his return to Scotland.

These and other exploits led to Rob becoming an almost legendary figure in his own lifetime. After ten years on the run, during which his many acts of generosity to the poor led to him becoming Scotland's Robin Hood, he did in the end submit himself to the government's well-known engineer General

Rob Roy MacGregor lies buried at Kirkton of Balquhidder, where devoted followers still often leave posies of flowers on his grave. Rob's wife and his two sons lie buried beside him. (Arthur Down)

Wade, of road- and bridge-building fame. Rob was subsequently granted the king's pardon.

In his latter years, Rob found comfort in the teachings of the Roman Catholic Church to which he became a convert. On the last day of January 1734 his adventurous life came to an end when he died at Inverlochlarig Beag at the top of the Glen of Balquhidder. As was the custom of the time, Rob's grave is marked by a simple, flat, table-top tombstone. Carved on it, very appropriately, are the words 'MacGregor Despite Them' and it is usually strewn with wreaths, bouquets and simple posies of flowers, left there by this Highland Robin Hood's many admirers, who come to pay their homage to him. The largest ever pilgrimage of members of the Clan MacGregor to Balquhidder took place a quarter of a century ago in 1975, when they gathered around the graveside of Rob and of his wife and two sons, who also lie buried in this lonely spot, to mark the 200th anniversary of the lifting of the proscription of their name MacGregor in 1775.

There are many other surnames which are linked to that of MacGregor. They include the obvious Gregor, Gregorson, Gregory, Greig, Grieg, Grierson and Grigor, but other septs or divisions of the MacGregor Clan also include Caird, Comrie, Crowther, Dochart (as in the name of the famous falls at Killin), Fletcher, King, Leckie, MacAdam (as in 'Tar' MacAdam fame), Macaree, Maconachie, MacNee, MacGruder, MacNeish, Malloch, Peter, Petrie, White and Whyte.

The MacGregor Clan badge is a gold lion's head topped with an antique crown, and the clan motto is the proud, 'Royal is my race!' Their clan plant is the pine and their nickname is 'The Children of the Mist' because they were said to be more adept than any others at taking advantage of the natural lie of the rugged Highland landscape in the Trossachs to disappear quickly and simply vanish from the scene. In addition to their lands throughout the Trossachs and in particular around Loch Lomond, Loch Katrine and Loch Voil in Balquhidder, they included Glendochart, Glen Lochy, Glen Orchy and Glen Strae and Rannoch Moor. The clan has several distinctive tartans, one of the most popular as befits these traditionally red-headed Highlanders being the colourful Modern Red MacGregor.

Rob Roy MacGregor's grave lies on the hillside just outside the ruined stone walls of the seventeenth-century Balquhidder kirk, which was gifted to the glen by Lord Scone in 1631. It was not, however, the original place of worship on this site because the foundations of an earlier kirk have also been discovered. This very early kirk is thought to date from the ninth century, when it was built over the grave of the Celtic St Angus. His tombstone survives and is now protected within the present place of worship.

The present kirk was a gift to the people of the glen from local laird David Carnegie of Stronvar who also gave the glen its school in 1869. Stronvar House, where he lived, is now available as a self-catering holiday home. Carnegie had made much of his wealth by investing in a brewery in Sweden, which deliberately produced a less potent beer to try to lessen the problem which that country had even in the nineteenth century with alcoholism. For a time Carnegie of Stronvar lived in Sweden and, when his son and heir died there aged only eight years old, this Scottish benefactor gave the Scandinavian country its first specialist children's hospital in Gothenburg, where a bronze bust of the little boy is still displayed in the entrance foyer.

Back at his home in the glen in 1855, Carnegie who could afford to employ over thirty servants to look after not only his own family, but also the many society guests he invited to stay during the shooting season each August and September, used some of his wealth to commission the well-known Scottish architect David Bryce to design a more comfortable place of worship to replace the seventeenth-century kirk, which was cold and draughty and falling into a state of disrepair. Balquhidder kirk was one of David Bryce's smaller commissions and he is more famous for his many Edinburgh city landmarks on which he employed his very distinctive Scottish baronial style. It is seen in all its glory in the towered and turreted façade of Edinburgh's historic former Royal Infirmary in the city centre. Bryce also designed the city's French château-like Fettes College, Scotland's most famous public school, of which Prime Minister Tony Blair is a former pupil.

At Balquhidder his design for the country kirk was far simpler, as befitted its setting, than either of these Edinburgh landmarks, but it is none the less appealing and worth visiting. Its interior includes the tombstone of St Angus. The font where baptisms take place is a simple rock from the hillside with a small hollow in to which the holy water is poured.

The kirk is also the resting place of the bell of the second church which originally hung in the stone birdcage belfry, which still tops its ruined, roofless gable wall, overlooking Rob Roy's grave. It was in fact used to call the faithful to worship in the present kirk for the first thirty years of its existence, until it cracked through old age in 1896. When taken down it was carefully preserved and remained in the kirk until 1973, when it was stolen. It was found in a scrapyard in Airdrie, Lanarkshire and now stands proudly once again in the kirk, displayed on top of an old oak kist. The bell was cast by Meikle of Edinburgh, whose mark of a thistle is inscribed upon it. Also engraved upon it are the words, 'For Balquhidder Church: Robert Kirk Minister: Love and Life: Anno 1684'. This was the same Revd Robert Kirk who later gained controversial notoriety as the minister of the parish of Aberfoyle, when, seven years later in 1691, he wrote his well-known book *The Secret Commonwealth of Elves, Fauns and Fairies*. In it he describes his meetings and conversations with the wee folk, who the following year are alleged to have spirited him away for revealing too many of their closely guarded secrets. His strange story is told in chapter seven.

It is appropriate to point out that he spent far longer ministering at Balquhidder than at Aberfoyle. This was his first charge after receiving his Doctor of Divinity degree from the University of St Andrews in 1664 when he was still only twenty years old. While at Balquhidder, as well as faithfully attending to his pastoral duties in his parish, whose territory then stretched all the way to the eastern shores of Loch Lomond, and preaching each Sunday, he also undertook much scholarly work, translating many of the psalms into Gaelic, and, as a result of his success in this task, he was commissioned to translate Bishop Bedale's Irish Bible into Gaelic. A copy of *Kirk's Bible in Gaelic* is displayed in Balquhidder kirk.

The Revd Robert Kirk's very distinguished record of theological research made his later book about Scotland's legendary little folk all the more talked about, because many of its readers refused to believe that a man so well versed in religious theory could possibly have resorted to fabricating such a detailed report or to have been duped in some way into writing it. Three centuries later, students of the supernatural are convinced that Kirk was genuine in his belief in the underworld and that perhaps he became more involved in it than any other person, before or after.

Those who are more sceptical wonder, however, if the sad event which marred the latter part of Mr Kirk's long ministry at Balquhidder could have had a greater effect on him than was imagined at the time, for his dearly loved wife, Isobel, the daughter of Sir Colin Campbell of Mochaster and the mother of his two children, died on Christmas Day 1680, when she was only twenty-five years old. The gravestone which he had erected in her memory can still be seen in the grounds of the kirk, but the ravages of the weather over the centuries have now unfortunately made it impossible to decipher the verses about his love for her carved upon it.

Today Balquhidder kirk still has a thriving congregation, who take a great pride and interest in it. Concerts are staged each summer during the annual music festival arranged in association with the charity organisation The Friends of Balquhidder, which aims to provide a platform for young musicians starting professional careers. Amongst those who have taken part since the Balquhidder Summer Music Festival began in 1986 are the now internationally renowned classical pianist Yonty Solomon, Australian guitarist Craig Ogden and the Telemann Ensemble. The concerts, which take place on Sunday evenings from the end of June until mid-August, are sponsored by the Gannochy Trust, the Royal Bank of Scotland, the McLaren Society and the Stirling Arts Forum.

Before leaving Balquhidder, explore further, as there is some most attractive scenery as the glen winds farther to the west along the shores of Loch Voil and beyond it to the smaller Loch Doine. Rising above the waters of Loch Voil are the Braes of Balquhidder, made famous in the folk song written by Robert Tannahill. The best viewpoint is Creagan Tuirc, from which the outlook is worth the climb. As in Brig O'Turk, Tuirc is derived from the Gaelic for wild boar and is a reminder that the Braes of Balquhidder were once amongst the best hunting lands in Scotland, a fact which had tragic consequences for the district.

The Glen of Balquhidder was originally the territory of the MacLaren Clan, but has also been associated with the Fergusons and the MacGregors for many centuries. It was here in 1589 that some MacGregor clansmen were caught poaching deer by the king's forester, John Drummond. They could not have chosen a worse time to be caught, as Drummond was under pressure to send as much venison to Edinburgh as possible for the triumphant banquet being

The nineteenth-century church of Balquhidder overlooks the ruins of the two earlier churches built on this site at Kirkton of Balquhidder. Behind it rise the famous Braes of Balquhidder. (Arthur Down)

planned to welcome home King James VI and his young bride, the Danish Princess Anne. Furious, Drummond had the ringleaders executed on the spot as the law of the time decreed for anyone caught robbing the monarch of his game. The lives of some of the MacGregors he spared, but punished them viciously by cutting off their ears and sending them home to warn their comrades of the consequences of further poaching.

His bloody warning had, however, the opposite effect on the MacGregors who, learning of the execution of their clansmen and the insulting punishment inflicted on those sent home to tell the tale, determined that in addition to continuing to catch the deer, the first thing they would catch would be Drummond himself. After days of patient hunting they at last tracked him down and had their terrible revenge by taking the royal servant captive. In their turn they then summarily put him to death in the most terrible fashion by tying him to his horse and dragging him along until every last breath was jolted out of his shattered body.

The MacGregor clansmen then swore an oath over Drummond's bloody, broken corpse, never to reveal who had executed him. Next they chopped off his head and carried it all the way to Ardvorlich House on the shores of Loch Earn. There they placed the decapitated head upon a silver salver and, with a crust of bread clasped between the luckless forester's bloodless lips, presented it to the Lady of Ardvorlich who, to make the deed even more repugnantly horrible, was his sister! At the time of this vile deed she was heavily pregnant and, in her shock and terror, she ran from the house and into the hills and hid in Glen Vorlich. There she was found in a distraught state by some of the local crofters, who had taken their cattle up to their summer pastures. Shortly afterwards she gave birth to a son, James Stewart, who later became known as the Mad Major. This nickname was acquired because of his cruel outbursts of temper, which gained him an evil reputation. It is said that he became the model for Sir Walter Scott's character Allan Macauley in *A Legend of Montrose*.

After they had terrified the Lady of Ardvorlich, the MacGregors carried the head of the forester back to Balquhidder and placed it upon the altar of the earliest of the churches which stood on the site. The Clan Chief, Alasdair MacGregor, summoned the whole clan and together they all solemnly agreed that none would betray the killers and that they would all share the blame. They did not have long to wait for the wrath of King James VI to descend upon them. The Lords of Council issued orders that the MacGregors were to be pursued 'with fire and sword' and amongst those who took up the chase was Stewart of Ardvorlich, the brother of the Lady of Ardvorlich. He and his men raided Balquhidder and caught and slew around thirty of the MacGregors.

The Commission of Fire and Sword meant that no MacGregor was safe. It commanded that any MacGregor clansman who was caught was to be tried on the spot and hanged, while his possessions were confiscated. Any of their womenfolk who dared come into any town and were spotted were to be arrested, stripped and their bare backs flogged.

King James VI maintained his persecution of the MacGregors even after the Union of the Crowns and his move south to London in 1603. To try to ease the situation, Clan Chief Alasdair tried to negotiate with the authorities, but was seized, arrested and thrown into Edinburgh's notorious Tolbooth Prison beside the High Kirk of St Giles in the High Street. There he was tried and executed on the spot where passers-by still show their disgust by spitting on the cobblestones which make up the Heart of Midlothian, from which Sir Walter Scott took the title for one of his Waverley Novels.

Despite such setbacks, the MacGregors fought back and survived. Sir Walter was always a fervent supporter of the MacGregors and in his poem 'MacGregors Gathering', he summed up their determination by writing, 'While there's leaves in the forest and foam on the river, MacGregor, despite them, shall flourish for ever'.

chapter three

The Trossachs Trail

From Balquhidder and its little-visited Loch Voil and Loch Doine, return to the much more frequently trekked Trossachs Trail, joining it at the old whitewashed toll house at Kilmahog on the northern outskirts of Callander. The projecting bay window, which allowed all approaching travellers to be spotted and where they had to stop to pay their dues before proceeding on their journeys, can still be seen. Today tolls are no longer collected at Kilmahog, but motorists should remember that they actually pay far more nowadays to travel these roads through road tax and the enormous and ever-increasing excise duty on petrol, which makes fuel in Scotland, despite its production of North Sea Oil and its refining of it at nearby Grangemouth, the most expensive in the world. Despite these vicious penalties, however, the beauty of this Trossachs Trail makes it one place where it truly feels worthwhile paying to enjoy driving along this scenic route.

Immediately after the road junction on the left lies the historic Lade Inn, whose food is recommended by Egon Ronay and praised by the AA, the *Wayside Inns* Guide, the *Which?* Guide and the *Britain's Best Pubs* Guide. Its range of Scottish beers is lauded by CAMRA, the Campaign for Real Ale, whose *Good Beer Guide* describes the quaint little Lade as 'a country pub as it should be', and in 2004 it established its own micro-brewery on the premises. The Lade's unusual name is, however, a reminder that before it was converted into such a pleasant little hostelry its links were not with beers, wines and spirits, but with good plain water. For it was originally a mill and the man-made lade carried the rushing waters of the river Leny to provide the power to turn its large wood and iron wheel, which in turn provided the motive force for the weaving looms.

The importance of water is brought to mind again a little further on by the sight of the long, low line of the solid stone-built Victorian waterworks, which stretch in a line across the eastern end of Loch Venachar. Venachar, whose name is derived from the Gaelic meaning The Fair Valley, begins 2¼ miles west of Callander and runs for 3¾ miles in a south-westerly direction. Situated at a height of 270ft above sea level, its waters flow into the river Teith. There is good

The old toll house still stands guardian at Kilmahog, where travellers used to have to pay their dues before continuing their journeys north to Crianlarich, south to Callander or west to the Trossachs. (Arthur Down)

trout fishing on it and boats may be hired from Venachar Fisheries, on the main A821 road which hugs its eastern shore.

In the past there was a ford on this road at the end of the loch. Coilantogle Ford, as it was known, has long been replaced by a bridge. It is, however, still deserving of mention for the sake of devotees of Sir Walter Scott, because it was there in his celebrated romantic poem 'The Lady of the Lake' that he set one of the most dramatic scenes, the defeat of Roderick Dhu, the Black Roderick, who was vanquished in single combat by the brave Fitz-James!

From fiction to fact, Queen Victoria also came to this tranquilly beautiful spot and was rowed across the waters of Loch Venachar when she spent a holiday touring the Trossachs in 1869 along with two of the royal princesses. Just before the start of the sparkling waters of the loch, a narrow side road to the left leads to Invertrossachs House on its west shore and it was here that the queen and her royal retinue took up residence for the several weeks which she spent enjoying touring the Trossachs. Right up until the news of the royal tour the mansion overlooking Loch Venachar was known as Drunkie House, after the other neighbouring loch, but in the spate of preparations for Her Majesty's visit, it was hurriedly decided that this name must be changed in case it caused offence to the queen's royal sensibilities! Thus Drunkie House became Invertrossachs House and has remained so ever since, but strangely little Loch Drunkie itself, which the queen saw on one of her outings during her stay, was allowed to keep its old Gaelic name, and to this day tour guides conducting their crowded bus parties through the Trossachs still tell them the tale that its title comes from an illicit whisky still, which was once operated on its shores.

Although there is no truth in the story, Loch Drunkie would certainly have been an excellent place to have quietly established such an illegal whisky-making enterprise to produce the potent 'moonshine', as it is well off the beaten track. Views of it can, however, be obtained by taking the Forestry Commission's Achray Forest Trail. Access to the trail is from the A821, the famous Duke's Road

The Brig O'Turk on a George
Washington Wilson photograph,
c.1870. (Alistair Deayton)

or Duke's Pass, which is described more fully in a later chapter. The Achray
Forest Trail is open seasonally from Easter until late autumn, providing an opportunity to drive along 7 miles of scenically spectacular Forestry roads.

Back down on the western shore of Loch Venachar, the entrance to the
Invertrossachs Estate is as far as vehicle access is allowed, but beyond the gate-
house there is pedestrian access to the Forestry Commission path which leads
over the Menteith Hills to Braeval on the outskirts of Aberfoyle, and this is a very
pleasant and not too strenuous half-day walk well worth taking.

For Queen Victoria, however, a horse-drawn carriage awaited after she
crossed Loch Venachar by boat and this carried her on west through the hamlet
of Brig O'Turk to the spot where she stopped to look out over its waters. The
scene is still known as the Queen's View and is every bit as picturesque and
unspoilt today as it was over a century ago, when it delighted Her Majesty.

Queen Victoria is often quoted as being 'not amused', but despite this it does
appear that she had a sense of humorous curiosity. Before her tour of the

Brig O'Turk Tearoom. (William F. Hendrie)

Trossachs, she had apparently heard of her royal realm's largest female inhabitant, who was the landlady of the inn at Brig O'Turk, and insisted on a special stop being included so that she could meet the enormous, twenty-four stone Kate Ferguson. For her royal audience Muckle Kate, as she was known, was dressed in her finest dress and shawl and is said to have enjoyed a conversation with the queen. Sadly details were not recorded, but the newspapers at the time did report that Muckle Kate was delighted that Her Majesty gave her two gold sovereigns and later descriptions of this unusual royal visit note that she treasured these £1 coins as her most precious possessions for the rest of her life. As landlady of the inn at Brig O'Turk, however, Muckle Kate was far from poor, as she ran a prosperous hostelry in a village that was then at its prime as a Victorian resort. At this time, and during the summer season, Brig O'Turk attracted many well-known artists, including the painters of the school known as the Glasgow Boys. It was also visited by John Everett Millais.

Nowadays, the Forestry Commission has created several small car parks and picnic sites along the shores of both Loch Venachar and Loch Achray, where modern visitors can pull off the narrow lochside to pause to enjoy the views, which the nineteenth-century artists painted in safety.

It is still, however, well worthwhile making a stop in Brig O'Turk itself, as it is a pleasant little place, with a collection of houses and cottages with colourful well-kept gardens, and an old stone bridge which leads the road across the waters of the river Turk. The village is the site of a rustic wooden tearoom, easily spotted driving west, but less easily seen coming from the other direction as it is tucked into the corner, where the side road leads up into Glen Finglas. For those who want something stronger to drink and more substantial fare to eat, the village is also the place to find the very popular Byre Inn, situated down a short drive into the forest. As well as its well-stocked bar, the Byre also offers a cosy pub restaurant.

The name Brig O'Turk is derived from the Gaelic meaning 'the place of the wild boar' and these ferocious little animals did indeed once roam the woodlands in this area; with their sharp, curved, pointed tusks, they were considered to provide the fiercest hunting available in Scotland. Brig O'Turk is, however, also a name which inevitably conjures up references to the mythical *Brigadoon*, the mysterious Highland village of Broadway musical fame which, according to Lerner and Loewe, emerged from the mists of time for one single day every hundred years, just long enough for New York-streetwise Tommy to fall in love with local lass Fiona.

In Brig O'Turk, however, such comparisons are not as far-fetched as they may at first seem, because the village is the location of a long-drowned Trossachs valley and the homes which stood there do occasionally still reappear when the water level falls during dry summers. To discover this drowned valley, take the little side road to the right in the middle of Brig O'Turk, which climbs steeply up into spectacular Glen Finglas. Back in the early 1960s it was decided to flood the glen, both to provide an extra supply of good fresh water for Glasgow and also to produce hydroelectricity. The result was the massive Glen Finglas Dam, which today spans the valley and behind which has been formed a 3-mile-long loch. On average the depth of water in this man-made loch is 95ft, but in places it is as deep as 200ft.

In 1960 the owner of the estate which formerly existed in the glen was paid £56,000 in compensation for his mansion house home and the neighbouring hamlet of shepherds' cottages. The shepherds and their flocks were all evacuated and the following year work began on the construction of the huge concrete dam. The project took four years to complete at a cost of approximately £1 million and resulted in a dam 100ft high and 100ft thick. There are four enormous valve pipes in the face of the wall of the dam and only one is used at a time. The valve which is opened draws 30 million gallons of water a day from the loch behind the dam and this lowers the level of the water by 4ins. Once the 30 million gallons of water have powered the electricity turbines, two thirds of the water goes by pipeline to Loch Katrine to boost Glasgow's water supply as described in a later chapter. The remaining 10 million gallons of water are returned as required by the Fisheries Board to maintain the level of water in the river Turk. As well as protecting fishing in the river, the scheme has also created brown trout fishing in the loch above.

Despite its size, Glen Finglas Dam has only ever had a staff of two employees. The two men are not employed on shifts as many people think. Both work daytime hours, with an alarm bell to alert them to anything which goes wrong at night and an automatic system which shuts down the whole operation in case of an emergency. For maintenance purposes there is an inspection tunnel so that the staff can check the wall along the base of the dam. The inspection tunnel is 62ft away from the water. It is used to check for seepage, which can be detected by looking for lime deposits. Calcium carbonate is dissolved in the water and this leaves a white deposit on the surface, similar to the material which creates stalactites and stalagmites in underground caves.

Trossachs Kirk. (William F. Hendrie)

There is also a vertical tunnel through the concrete of the dam. It climbs up to the building at the end of the observation walkway on the top of the dam, which is used to house equipment for cleaning the front of the dam wall and clearing away any branches of trees or other debris which threatens to block the entrances to any of the four valve pipes. A plaque, marking the official opening of the Glen Finglas Project, is sited at the top of the path leading to the observation walkway.

When the loch behind the dam is full, water often overflows and crashes down. This is why concrete steps have been constructed; they break up the flow of the water and thus take the pressure of the water off the wall of the dam, which might otherwise be damaged. At the other extreme, when the water level of the loch falls during a long dry spell, it is perhaps at its most interesting, because it is then that, in true *Brigadoon* fashion, the hamlet of drowned houses reappears into sight. The roofs of the houses were removed before the glen was flooded, but even a glimpse of their walls is quite an eerie sight. Unfortunately it is one which few people have the opportunity to see, because this ingenious project is not open to the public.

Back down in Brig O'Turk the A821 road continues west along the shores of Loch Achray, which, translated from the Gaelic, has the rather strange meaning of 'the smooth field'. The 'smooth' part of its name, however, perhaps helps explain why it is a popular venue for watersports including waterskiing. All the way the road skirts the water's edge, providing first-rate views out across its waters to the hills beyond, but equally creating hazards for any driver who is momentarily distracted. The lochside road is so narrow that there is little room for passing and when two of the large touring coaches meet, as they often do, their drivers have a very tricky task inching their huge vehicles slowly past each other to the terror of their passengers. In winter the road past Loch Achray is often equally treacherous as the loch waters flood across its surface to the depth of a foot or more.

At the far end of 1¼-mile-long Loch Achray comes one of its most photographed views: the tiny stone-built Trossachs Kirk. Situated on the top of a little hill, it has featured on the pages of many calendars. The kirk, which was opened in 1849, is still in use, with services on occasional Sundays especially during the summer, and there can be few more lovely spots in the world in which to worship. Trossachs Kirk is linked to the Church of Scotland in Callander, with the minister travelling out to serve its scattered congregation.

For relaxing and holidaying, Loch Achray is a delightful spot, a fact which has been recognised for many years since the construction of the impressively turreted, grey slate-roofed, thick stone-walled, four-storey-high Trossachs Hotel. Constructed in 1852, it has recently been immaculately restored as the An Tigh Mor, managed by Holiday Property Bond of Newmarket, Suffolk. An Tigh Mor is Gaelic for The Big House and it fits this description well as it rises château-like above the loch. Its tall slate-clad towers, however, give this château a distinctly Scottish baronial appearance and this is indeed exactly the impression which it was intended to create, for it was built specifically to cater for the demand for Scottish holidays resulting from Queen Victoria and Prince Albert's choice of Balmoral on Royal Deeside as their annual summer holiday hideaway. Suddenly 'huntin', shootin', fishin' and sight-seein'' in Scotland was very much the 'in' thing to do.

Fortunately, at precisely the right time, the coincidence of the construction of the railways made it possible for the English upper and middle classes to invade the Highlands, of which the area of the Trossachs was the nearest and easiest to reach. With its sweeping drive and almost as vast interior with its ballroom, dining room and winter gardens conservatory, the new Trossachs Hotel was

The entrance to the Trossachs Hotel in a hard winter during the 1920s. (J. & C. McCutcheon)

offered as the ideal place to stay. Its lavishly printed and worded brochure promised guests that its fleet of horse-drawn brakes and charabancs would transport them daily to connect with the new-fangled paddle steamers on Loch Katrine and Loch Lomond and to view all of the area's more distant attractions, while local walks included the dramatic climb up Ben An, with its volcano-like outline.

Ben An is the type of mountain which simply demands to be climbed, and fortunately the Forest Enterprise has provided a conveniently situated car park right at its foot. From there, for those who have the energy, the 1,851ft-high summit of Ben An is comparatively easy to reach as a rough path leads all the way to the top. Its name in Gaelic means The Pinnacle and that well describes its dramatically jagged outline. From the craggy summit there is a spectacular view down to the narrow pass, from which the Trossachs originally derived its name and then on out over the waters of Loch Katrine, which is our next port of call.

Left The very Scottish baronial-style Trossachs Hotel, with its four tall pepper-pot towers, was built in 1852 to cater for the growing number of Victorian tourists who followed the example of Queen Victoria and her royal consort Prince Albert and came to holiday in Scotland. This view shows the hotel in 1870 before its many extensions. (Alistair Deayton)

Top Looking down on to Loch Achray and Ben Venue in 1870. (Alistair Deayton)

Above Looking towards Ben Venue in the 1870s. (Alistair Deayton)

chapter four

The Lady of the Loch

The connection between an outbreak of the dreaded disease cholera in Scotland's largest city, Glasgow, and the sparkling, clear, pure waters of Loch Katrine may not seem obvious immediately, but there is one and it greatly altered the scenery in this part of the Trossachs. It was the devastating spread of cholera throughout Glasgow in 1848 which persuaded the city's Lord Provost and his fellow bailies and councillors that they must prevent any such occurrence in the future by obtaining the purest possible source of fresh water for its citizens.

At the beginning of the nineteenth century, Glasgow's population of 85,000 people depended solely on thirty public wells and a very few private ones for their water supply. There was no piped supply and water had to be collected in pails and jugs from the wells in the streets. The quality of the water was so poor that those families who could afford it gladly paid for water supplied by private companies, who brought in large wooden barrels from the surrounding countryside and delivered it to the city centre and surrounding districts by horse-drawn cart. The water was then sold at a penny a jug.

Even for those who could afford the luxury of buying this barrelled water, there was no guarantee of its purity and, after many complaints, the city fathers therefore decided that drastic action was necessary to improve the situation. In 1853 they voted to take the water supply under municipal control and commissioned an English civil engineer, John Frederick Bateman, to find the best possible source of water for the city.

Bateman travelled north and spent much of the following year exploring all possible sources of water around the city, before recommending his ambitious scheme to pipe in the water all the way from Loch Katrine – because its waters were so pure and its drainage area so large and unpolluted – by means of a 26-mile-long aqueduct. Such a colossal project might well have daunted any other municipality, but Glasgow was then the extremely prosperous second city of the whole of the British Empire and so the Lord Provost and his supporters courageously agreed to back Bateman's scheme.

In April 1855 Glasgow Corporation promoted a Bill in the House of Commons and obtained permission to construct a stone dam to increase the water level of the loch and to link it by aqueduct to Mugdock Reservoir at Milngavie. From there a further 26 miles of large trunk pipes and 46 miles of smaller distribution pipes would carry the pure, fresh water from Loch Katrine to virtually every home and business in the city by gravity, apart from one small area where pumping would be required.

As soon as the Act of Parliament promoting the Glasgow Water Works Scheme was passed, no time was lost and the massive project was completed in only three and a half years. It was considered such a wonderful feat of engineering that nothing less than a royal opening was justified and the Lord Provost and magistrates were delighted when Queen Victoria and Prince Albert accepted their invitation to perform the ceremony at Stronachlachar, and no expense was spared to make the occasion the most spectacular ever seen in the west of Scotland.

On the morning of 14 October 1859 the royal train steamed into the railway station at Callander. When the queen and Prince Albert disembarked onto the platform they stepped out through a triumphant arch covered in eye-catching scarlet Royal Stewart tartan and purple heather. It was the first of a whole series of similar arches, which were erected along the route to the Trossachs Pier. The route was also specially marked with distinctive white and black cast-iron mile posts and several of these survive along the roadside to this day.

Travelling by coach, Victoria and Albert were accompanied on their royal progress by a detachment of splendidly liveried cavalry. Sadly the excited watching crowd saw little of the eye-catching uniforms, however, because the horsemen had to wear their capes, as the only thing which was not splendid that autumn day was the weather. Somewhat ironically for the opening of a new waterworks, the heavens opened and torrential rain poured down.

The atrocious weather, however, did not deter the crowds and thousands awaited the royal party's arrival at Trossachs Pier. There they were greeted by a noise like thunder, but it was actually a twenty-one-gun salute, whose ear-shattering salvoes echoed back from the slopes of Ben Venue. As the thunderous noise subsided the royal couple were formally welcomed by the Lord Provost of Glasgow, who was accompanied by all of his bailies and other magistrates and their wives. The bailies and magistrates almost out-dazzled their ladies because they all wore their scarlet, ermine-trimmed gowns, which made them stand out from the remaining councillors and other distinguished guests in their more sombre black morning suits and tall silk top hats.

The royal party, civic leaders and invited guests then all embarked on the new steamer, *Rob Roy II*, for the forty-five-minute sail to Stronachlachar. There, the queen disembarked at the pier and, despite the soaking wet weather, declined the opportunity to proceed under the cover of the canopied walkway to the tented pavilion, insisting instead on keeping to the original plan, and was therefore helped into the waiting small open boat and, to the delight of the vast crowd, was rowed the final short distance along the shore of the loch to the point where she was to perform the opening ceremony. The two oarsmen were well-known local boatmen, John MacDonald and Peter MacGregor, who was a descendant of the famous outlawed Rob.

The queen was assisted ashore on the banks of the loch at the appropriately named Royal Cottage, which had been specially built for the occasion. Solidly built of local stone, it still stands overlooking the loch and to the right of it can be seen the sluices, which Her Majesty opened for the first time to send thousands of gallons of water flooding through the tunnels and stone aqueducts constructed to take them all the way to Milngavie on the northern outskirts of Glasgow. As the rain continued, the queen and Prince Albert were escorted into Royal Cottage, where they were entertained to lunch. The opening of the waterworks was such an important event that a detailed drawing of the opening appeared in the pages of the following week's *London Illustrated News*.

From then on, every year the Glasgow officials insisted in reliving the big day, on the excuse that they would be failing in their duty if they did not conduct an annual inspection of their waterworks, but the occasion became more associated with the consumption of whisky than of the product of the loch. By the time of the golden anniversary of Queen Victoria's accession to the throne, this annual civic bun fight had grown into a two-day affair.

That summer a minister from St Andrews, the Revd Mr Lyons, was acting as locum, relieving the resident minister in Callander, and was invited to join in the festivities when the official party from Glasgow reached the town on the evening of the first day. He wrote:

This view from 1870 shows the area near the boat pier before the water level of Loch Katrine was increased in 1895. (Alistair Deayton)

> On the evening of Thursday July 7th, I was invited to the famous Dreadnought Hotel, to dine with the Magistrates of Glasgow, making their annual inspection of their magnificent water-works. About a hundred were present; a most cordial and pleasant set of men. The Lord Provost, Sir James King, presided and I was much interested to meet Mr Underwood, the American Consul at Glasgow. He was the first editor of the *Atlantic Monthly*. I was most impressed by the excellence of the after-dinner speeches. The Glasgow hospitality was magnificent. The large party had spent that day in tracing the water-works all the way from Glasgow and I was invited to join them the following morning on the continuation of their journey to the water's source at Loch Katrine. And so, at 8 a.m., I returned to the Dreadnought for a hearty breakfast, which set us up well for the day ahead. We set off in three/four horse coaches, while the Lord Provost, the Consul and my unworthy self, went ahead of the procession in a carriage and pair. It was the brightest of days and we admired Loch Venachar and the Trossachs in all their glory. Refreshments awaited us at the Trossachs Pier, where we boarded the steamer to sail the length of Loch Katrine. At Stronachlachar other coaches were waiting to convey the party to Inversnaid on Loch Lomond, where they again joined the steamer to sail down the Queen of Lochs to Balloch and back to Glasgow by railway. I went a little way on one of the coaches along the road to Inversnaid, but had sorrowfully to turn back to await the arrival of the afternoon steamer at Stronachlachar. While I waited, I sat on a rock overlooking Loch Katrine and wrote a letter to the *Scotsman*.

Everyone knows that that newspaper is published in Edinburgh and that there is a certain jealousy between the two greatest cities of Scotland, but my letter praising the Lord Provost, Magistrates and Town Councillors of the great city of Glasgow, whom I had met on the water-works journey, as the pleasantest, cleverest and kindest set of men, duly appeared in print, the following Monday morning. In a few days various letters reached me, approving of my sentiments and the next year, when the water-works came to be inspected, the kindest of all kind invitations brought me to accompany the expedition from first to last!

Since the original damming of its waters, the surface level of Loch Katrine has been raised a further three times by Acts of Parliament to meet the increasing demands of the city. Now it is on average 17ft above its original height and the loch's own supply is supplemented by thousands of additional gallons each day from neighbouring Loch Arklet, which was dammed in 1885, and more recently since the 1960s, by supplies from Glen Finglas, which are transported by underground tunnel from Brig O'Turk.

An 1885 Act of Parliament also gave permission for the construction of a second draw-off basin at Royal Cottage together with a second aqueduct and an additional storage reservoir at Craigmaddie near Milngavie, plus extra trunk mains pipes and more distribution pipes in further parts of the ever-expanding city. The total amount of water which can be stored is enough to keep the people of Glasgow supplied for over half a year.

The diameter of both aqueducts is 10ft and they are linked throughout their length so that maintenance work can be carried out without interruption to the supply. Each aqueduct can carry 85 million gallons a day and the amount required from both each day totals 120 million gallons, giving plenty of spare capacity. To protect the purity and quality of the water, Glasgow Corporation bought all of the water catchment area around Loch Katrine and Loch Arklet and they have been guarded jealously ever since. The water is so pure that there is very little need for treatment at the Milngavie Waterworks, which simply passes it through straining screens and adds some quantities of lime to neutralise acidity, phosphate to reduce lead and chlorine as a disinfectant.

So pure in fact has the water from Loch Katrine always been that it resulted in an unexpected health problem for the city. During the early years of the twentieth century, it was discovered that many Glasgow children were what was described as 'bandie leggit' because they were suffering from rickets, a bone disease caused by a deficiency of calcium, there being none in the water from the loch. This is because millions of years ago violent earthquakes and upheavals in the area now occupied by the Trossachs resulted in the sedimentary rocks being metamorphosed and the calcium in them being burnt off. The extent of this upheaval way back in geological times can still be seen by examining the rocks in the narrow pass leading to Trossachs Pier. The health problem amongst Glasgow's bairns was solved by ensuring that mothers in the city took additional supplies of calcium during their pregnancies.

Left The Silver Strand, Loch Katrine, in 1870 (Alistair Deayton)

Right The 'Path by the Loch' in 1870 made famous in Sir Walter Scott's 'The Lady of the Lake'. (Alistair Deayton)

The other drawback to the use of Loch Katrine as the source of Glasgow's water supply was, of course, that the increased water level meant that some of its famous views and scenic attractions were either altered or drowned. Such was the fate of the famous sands which made up the Silver Strand near Trossachs Pier, celebrated by Sir Walter Scott in 'The Lady of the Lake'. Opposite where the beach used to be, Ellen's Isle, or Eilean Molach to give it its original Gaelic name, was also greatly reduced in size, but is still a reminder of when it was larger and acted as a convenient place of refuge for the women and children of the MacGregor Clan if it seemed likely that they might be attacked.

While the womenfolk and children were sheltered on Ellen's Isle, the MacGregors also had a hideaway for their cattle, many of them allegedly stolen, which they grazed on the small peninsula known as the Prison, as they could be guarded by only one man. The cattle hidden away there were driven through the Pass of the Cattle at the foot of Ben Venue, the highest of the mountain peaks to the south of the loch. Just below the Pass, through which the cattle were herded, lies the Cave of the Goblins, which is reputedly haunted by the wee folk of the district. The goblins, elves and brownies were supposedly forced to make their home in this isolated spot after being made to leave the lowlands to the south of the Menteith Hills, along the shores of the Lake of Menteith, by order of the Prior of Inchmahome.

Ellen's Isle, 1870. (Alistair Deayton)

It is alleged that it was one of the wicked goblins, who caused the loch to acquire its name. According to local legend he was furious when his amorous advances were rejected by the beautiful virgin maiden who guarded a fountain which flowed from below the surface of Ben Venue and provided the clearest, purest water in the whole of Scotland. Her name is variously given as Catherine, Katherine or Katrine and when in a rage the goblin caused her fountain to over-flow, she was drowned in the waters of the loch which was formed and which now, of course, bears her name. Certainly 8-mile-long Loch Katrine, which is situ-ated 364ft above sea level and which reaches a depth of 78 fathoms, around 468ft, is still as generously fed with sparkling pure water as in the days of the virgin maiden's fountain, as it is supplied by forty-eight streams flowing down from the surrounding hills of which Ben Venue is undoubtedly the most impressive.

While the slopes of Ben Venue are said to be inhabited by many of Scotland's wee folk, both good and evil, human habitations around the shores of Loch Katrine are very few and far between because successive water boards have not allowed any new homes to be built. The most developed area is at Trossachs

Pier. There the largest building is a very Victorian-looking two-storey tearoom. Stone built, it has a steeply sloping slate roof and a castellated tower. This rather eccentric structure is now known equally strangely as the Captain's Table and caters for visitors throughout the season from the beginning of April until the beginning of October. Further along the car park, away from the loch, two former semi-detached water workers' houses have been converted into a visitor centre and, at the pier head, a former stone-built boathouse has been turned into a souvenir shop. The stone ramp up which the small rowing boats used for trout fishing on the loch used to be pulled out of the water, can still be seen. Before leaving this area and passing through the iron railings to reach the road, which leads round the north shore of Loch Katrine, pause to enjoy a refreshing sample of loch water from the stone-built drinking fountain.

Motor traffic on the narrow road round the north shore is limited to official water board vehicles and private cars are not allowed, but it is possible to walk or cycle right round the head of the loch to Stronachlachar from where roads lead on to Inversnaid on Loch Lomond and to Aberfoyle. Bicycle hire is available at the pier and a limited number of cycles can be transported on the *Sir Walter Scott.*

For those who prefer to pedal away from the pier and cycle round the loch on the narrow road which follows its northern shore all the way to Stronachlachar, the first feature of interest is the point where the water pumped through the tunnel from Glen Finglas floods into the loch. It is a spectacular sight as it crashes out into the calm waters of the loch. Equally worth a halt are the views from this point across the loch to the towering slopes of Ben Venue.

The first house passed on the journey round the loch is the imposing-looking Brenachoile Lodge. A nineteenth-century mansion, it was originally used as a shooting lodge before it was purchased by Glasgow Water Board in 1920. There are also three farms on the north shore: Lettre, Edra and Strone. Before the

Bedford OB Duple coaches at Trossachs Pier, c.1955.

Industrial Revolution in Scotland in the late eighteenth century, iron-making was a small rural enterprise because of the requirement for wood to make charcoal for the smelting process, and near Strone Farm are the remains of one of several small foundries to be found around the loch. The site is marked by cinders and charcoal, showing where the ore was smelted to extract the iron.

Looking across the loch beyond Strone Farm there are clear views of Royal Cottage. On the northern side the road hugs the shore and the next feature of interest is the little graveyard at Portmellan, where several members of Clan MacGregor lie buried. Portmellam is Gaelic for The Port of the Island and true enough just offshore lies the Black Isle. The stone wall surrounding Portmellan was constructed to protect the graves from the water level of the loch.

Not far beyond the graveyard is situated a house, which is of most historic interest in the area. This is Glengyle, where Rob Roy MacGregor was born. From there it is only a short distance to the head of the loch and the road then follows the west shore for about 3 miles back south to Stronachlachar, which, after Trossachs Pier, is the next most developed spot on the loch. Stronachlachar means the Mason's Nose or Point and it is believed that it takes its name from the fact that a stone mason did have his home there at one time. Today it is the site of the stone-and-wood-built pier, where the steamer berths and also where the slipway marks where she was originally launched. The slipway is still in use, as this is where the steamer is removed from the water at the end of each autumn for the winter season.

At the head of the pier at Stronachlachar is a long, low Victorian building which provides a waiting room and toilets for those waiting for the steamer. The little shop and post office which once operated from this same building have long since closed, but there is still a traditional red telephone kiosk, a postbox, visited each day by the post bus from Aberfoyle, and, rather incongruously in this lonely outpost of civilisation, a vending machine dispensing cold drinks.

Stronachlachar is also the headquarters for the West of Scotland Water Board's operation at Loch Katrine and, beyond the iron-railed oval of evergreen shrubs, the road leads past its impressive red and cream mansion-like offices and other buildings. In Victorian times there was also a hotel at Stronachlachar.

Just offshore lies another of the islands in the loch. It is known as Factor's Island and it takes its name from the fact that it was here that Rob Roy imprisoned the Duke of Montrose's estate factor. Rob relieved the poor factor of all of the estate rents which he was carrying and then added insult to injury by demanding that his sworn enemy the Duke pay a handsome ransom for the release of his ill-fated servant! Like Portmellan on the opposite shore, Factor's Island has been well protected by the construction of high stone dykes to protect it from flooding due to the increased level of the loch. Landing on Factor's Island is not permitted, but excellent close-up views of it can be had from the decks of the steamer as she departs from the pier.

From Stronachlachar the shore road leads on to Royal Cottage and the waterworks there, but this is a dead end and the choice is therefore either to return

In the wheel house of the SS *Sir Walter Scott*. From right to left are her former skipper, Captain John Fraser, First Officer Neil McKenzie and Chief Engineer Raymond Howells, who is now captain. (William F. Hendrie)

to Trossachs Pier, or to take the road past Loch Arklet to Inversnaid on Loch Lomond or to drive to Aberfoyle.

Alternatively, visitors can catch the once-a-day sailing of the *Sir Walter Scott*, but this needs some logistical planning, as the fact that the steamer does not make a return call means that sailing from this end of the loch will mean returning to Stronachlachar by road via Aberfoyle. As the trip on the steamer is definitely the best way to view Loch Katrine, the best plan is to join the *Sir Walter Scott* on her daily morning sailing from Trossachs Pier and stay on board for the whole round trip. The *Sir Walter* sails daily except Saturdays from Trossachs Pier at 11.00 a.m. and returns at approximately 12.45 p.m. *Sir Walter* also provides two shorter afternoon cruises every day during the season from the beginning of April until October and, apart from the splendid views from her open decks, she is very much a tourist attraction in her own right as she is the only surviving steam screw steamer sailing in British waters and in October 1999 celebrated her centenary on the loch.

Sir Walter is, however, by no means the first passenger vessel to ply the waters of Loch Katrine. The earliest pleasure trips were provided by the *Water Witch*, which took its name from one of the legendary figures said to haunt the shores of the loch. The *Water Witch* was a sturdy eight-oared wooden galley and she was introduced to cater for the steadily growing number of visitors who wanted to view the scenic beauty of the loch as a result of the publication of Sir Walter Scott's romantic poem 'The Lady of the Lake'.

As well as showing all of their early Victorian passengers the wonders of the loch so vividly described by Sir Walter in his celebrated verses, the wily Highlanders who manned the *Water Witch* also always kept them very happy and ensured extra tips by including a visit to Jonathon's Island. Officially this was to allow them to enjoy a sample of the milk which Jonathon kept on the island, but this was only an excuse to fool the local gauger or excise man, because the recluse had actually established an illicit still and was happy to sell them his high-proof moonshine whisky. The first raising of the waters of the loch in 1859 submerged the little island where this enterprising character lived. It now lies below the surface close to the south shore.

In 1843 the livelihood of the oarsmen who propelled the old *Water Witch* was suddenly threatened by the arrival of the first paddle steamer to offer excursions on Loch Katrine. Built on the river Forth at Stirling, the little PS *Gypsy* was transported by road to the loch and successfully launched. The service which she provided was, however, short lived, because the oarsmen, furious at being made redundant by this new-fangled rival, crept aboard in the middle of the night and scuttled her. The *Gypsy* was never salvaged and her wreck still lies on the bottom of the loch.

The *Water Witch* had the waters of Loch Katrine to herself again in 1844, but her crew could not halt the march of progress and the following year another paddle steamer, the appropriately named *Rob Roy*, arrived and survived to provide a regular service of pleasure cruises until the end of the 1850s. This time she was built not on the Forth, but on the river Clyde by the famous shipbuilding yard belonging to William Denny & Bros Ltd. She was small enough to sail from Dumbarton up the river Leven to Balloch on Loch Lomond from where she sailed north as far as Inversnaid. There, she was dismantled and her parts carried over land on horse-drawn carts to Stronachlachar, where she was rebuilt and launched on Loch Katrine.

In 1850 Britain's earliest travel agent, the famous Thomas Cook, introduced a tour of the Trossachs into his ever-expanding list of itineraries. What must have been one of the very first package tours of the Trossachs was fully booked and Cook decided to mark the occasion by entrusting his son John, who was still only a teenager, with being courier and guide for the hundred participants. The journey was very complicated for the young man to organise, involving trains, horse-drawn wagonettes and steamers, and unfortunately almost everything which could go wrong did. The weather was atrocious, the trains delayed and one of the coaches suffered a broken wheel. The result was that when the bedraggled party finally arrived at Trossachs Pier for what was billed to be the highlight of the whole tour, John discovered to his horror that the *Rob Roy* had sailed without them. Undeterred he commandeered all of the rowing boats used in those days by fishermen on the loch, divided the members of his party amongst them and set off to row up the loch. No sooner had they left Trossachs Pier, however, when the weather worsened. A sudden squall blew up, sending waves across the usually placid surface of the water. Packed with far more people than it usually carried on its trout fishing trips, one of the little rowing boats was swamped and its occupants almost drowned before being rescued by the other vessels. John Cook never forgot this adventure on Loch Katrine and many years later it even featured in his obituary, which recorded that, 'the journey was only completed through that unconquerable resolve to keep faith with the public, which has ever since been one of the best traditions of his firm.'

Despite the difficulties of early tourism, however, throughout the period of service of the first *Rob Roy* on the loch the number of visitors continued to grow.

Left Before the SS *Sir Walter Scott*, a steamer with an equally famous name sailed the waters of Loch Katrine. This was the SS *Rob Roy*, as shown here in 1870. (Alistair Deayton)

Right The SS *Rob Roy* at Stronachlachar pier in 1870. This pier is actually Coalbarns, the first pier at Stronachlachar. It and the adjacent hotel were both abandoned when the water levels were increased in 1895. (Alistair Deayton)

As a result, by the close of the 1850s it was decided by the Loch Katrine Steamship Co. Ltd to replace her with a larger vessel of the same name. This time, instead of a paddle steamer the new *Rob Roy* was the first screw-propelled vessel to sail on the loch. Her funnel was carefully positioned towards the stern so that any smuts of soot were blown away and this improvement together with her sleek yacht-like lines made her a great favourite with passengers. She continued to cruise until 1900. During her final season she cruised in tandem with the new *Sir Walter Scott*. When finally withdrawn from service, *Rob Roy II* was laid up in the bay just to the west of the present boarding place at Trossachs Pier, where the remains of her boiler could still be seen until recent years.

By the time that the Loch Katrine Steamship Co. Ltd were considering replacing the second *Rob Roy* in the late 1890s, Victorian tourism was at its peak and it was therefore decided to order the largest vessel which these waters have ever seen. This time, rather strangely, the order was placed not with a ship-builder, but with the Dumbarton engineering firm of M. Paul & Co., who were to provide the steam engines for the new vessel, but they in turn simply solved the little problem of who was to build her by immediately subcontracting the job to the experienced William Denny & Bros Ltd shipbuilding yard at Dumbarton on the shores of the River Clyde to construct her at their nearby yard.

SS *Sir Walter Scott* ties up at the pier on 19 June 1964. In 1956 her saloon windows were replaced by the portholes shown here. As well as supplying Glasgow with its water from Loch Katrine, the Water Board operates the SS *Sir Walter Scott* on the loch and has ensured its water is kept absolutely pure by maintaining the ship as a coal-fired steamer and refusing to convert her to diesel, which might cause pollution. (J. & C. McCutcheon)

Order number 623, placed with Paul's on 20 February 1899, stated that the new vessel was to be 'an excursion passenger launch' and stipulated that she was 'to be ready for next year's season'. While Paul's busied themselves building a triple-expansion engine, work got underway on the shores of the Clyde with the construction of the new ship. Her steel hull was 110ft long and 19ft wide. This meant that she was too large to sail through the river Leven to Loch Lomond and so as soon as she was completed all of her parts were carefully numbered and she was then dismantled again. This was a practice at which Denny Bros were expert, as they had previously built several steamers for the rivers and lakes of Africa which had been delivered in what was known as knockdown kit form, and the new vessel for Loch Katrine was very similar in size and indeed in appearance with her open teak decks and striped linen awnings.

Once dismantled, the pieces of the new Loch Katrine steamer were loaded into large wooden crates. These were placed on a barge which was then towed from Denny Bros' yard up the river Leven and on up the length of Loch Lomond once again to Inversnaid. There the crates were loaded onto horse-drawn carts, which hauled them the 5 miles across country to Stronachlachar. There she was swiftly reconstructed on the shores of the loch, where the slipway still marks the spot, and on 31 October 1899 was launched as the *Sir Walter Scott*.

Excluding the cost of her engine and the two coal-fired boilers required to power it, Denny Bros had quoted £4,250 as their price for the new vessel. The final bill rendered to the Loch Katrine Steamship Co. Ltd for the *Sir Walter,* including £2,028 for delivery, was £4,269. Apart from this slight excess charge, the *Sir Walter* has enjoyed a very happy century of service on Loch Katrine and she is now the only surviving screw-propelled steamer sailing in British waters.

The *Sir Walter* was equipped with a triple-expansion engine with three cylinders of 8½ins, 13ins and 19ins diameter, by 12in stroke. Her two boilers were

With her decks crowded with holidaymakers, SS *Sir Walter Scott* draws into the pier at Stronachlachar, the northern terminus of her morning cruise on Loch Katrine. (Joan Down)

similar to those installed on railway locomotives, with a working pressure of 160lbs per square inch.

The original plans for the *Sir Walter* can be seen in a display at Trossachs Pier and it is interesting to note that the loch was considered so remote that originally cabins were provided so that all the members of her six-man crew could sleep onboard. Later the captain and crew were accommodated ashore at a hostel built near Trossachs Pier. Nowadays they all go home at night and an alarm is fitted aboard the *Sir Walter* to warn them of any danger.

Like all passenger vessels plying for business in British waters, the *Sir Walter* has to conform to very strict regulations laid down by the Board of Trade and at the beginning of every season she is checked by its inspectors. When she first began sailing on the loch the *Sir Walter*'s certificate to operate as a passenger vessel stated that she was licensed to carry 416 passengers. Over the years alterations and increased safety requirements, including the provision of inflatable lifesaving rafts in addition to her single lifeboat in the stern, have reduced this number and she now caters comfortably for around 320 passengers with a ship's company of five.

Captain of the *Sir Walter*, Raymond Howells, was formerly the vessel's chief engineer. He began his engineering career as a car mechanic working for the well-known Northampton firm of Cosworth on whose racing cars he gained his experience. Mr Howells had no particular interest in steam engines until he spotted the advertisement for the post of engineer aboard the *Sir Walter*. His first season aboard the ship was in 1997 and although her boilers had been renewed by N.E.I. Cochran of Annan in 1991, who replaced the originals with those of a modified steam locomotive type, he discovered that the steam engine itself was very much in need of a complete overhaul.

By this time, the *Sir Walter* was under the new ownership of West of Scotland Water, and the superintendent with responsibility for the vessel, Allan Fall, arranged that the overhaul should be undertaken as soon as possible at the end of the season. This involved winching the 4-ton engine out of the tiny engine room aboard the *Sir Walter* and transporting it to the headquarters of the *Waverley* paddle steamer at Finnieston Quay in Glasgow. There some of Scotland's leading steam enthusiasts worked on the engine throughout the winter, finally testing that all was well by running it on compressed air.

The beautifully restored engine was then transported by road back to Trossachs Pier, where a 20-ton mobile crane was brought in to gently lower it back into the hull of the *Sir Walter*. Although the engine is exactly as it was built a century ago by Paul's of Dumbarton, since 1967 it has been fired not with coal but with a reactive solid smokeless fuel called Coalite. Although only converted to burn this solid fuel thirty years ago, it is interesting to note that Coalite is in fact almost as old as the *Sir Walter* as it was discovered in the early years of the 1900s by the English inventor Thomas Park. Unlike the lake steamers on Windermere and other inland waters in England, the *Sir Walter* has escaped conversion to diesel because of the fear that oil pollution might contaminate the drinking water supplied to the people of Glasgow from the loch.

In 1989 the *Sir Walter*'s unique place in steam history was recognised by the British Coal and Solid Fuel Advisory Service through the presentation of the Steam Service Premium Award, which is displayed onboard the vessel.

Now restored to all of her former glory, the *Sir Walter* looks set to sail on well into the Millennium, backed by the most ambitious public relations exercise which the little ship has ever known. Imaginative marketing plans, both afloat and ashore, include the employment of actors to play the parts of well-known people who have figured in the history of the Trossachs, from Rob Roy MacGregor to Sir Walter Scott, and to help bring alive the stories and legends of the district. The steamer is also being offered for evening charters for corporate entertainment and to this end a licence to dispense drinks has been obtained for the first time, because although in her early days the *Sir Walter* boasted an excellent dining saloon, she never had a bar.

The *Sir Walter Scott*'s career has also included featuring in a film about emigration to Canada and the filming onboard of a Johnny Cash Christmas television special. With with her photogenic appearances, she is in ever-increasing demand for the shooting of television commercials and these have gained her welcome publicity in countries ranging from Japan to America. Several wedding receptions have also been held onboard, but Captain Howells stresses that he does not have the authority to perform marriage ceremonies on the bridge.

All in all a voyage on the *Sir Walter Scott* is always brimful of interest, from staring down at the flaming orange glow of her fire in the engine room, to standing *Titanic*-like poised on her bows as Captain Howells orders full steam ahead and she ploughs up the loch at all of 8 knots. But who would desire to travel faster, for a cruise aboard the *Sir Walter* is something to linger over and enjoy as this hundred-year-old vessel helps recreate the spirit of the Victorian age.

chapter five

The Duke's Pass

From the end of Loch Katrine at Trossachs Pier, the way to Aberfoyle is by one of Scotland's most famous high-level hill roads, the Duke's Pass. This popular tourist route takes its name from the Duke of Montrose, Rob Roy MacGregor's sworn enemy, who originally built this twisting, turning hill road to enable his coach horses to tackle the steep gradients and enable him to reach his hunting lodge on the shores of Loch Achray.

The Loch Achray Hotel now stands on the site and incorporates some remnants of the original hunting lodge. Like many other hotels in the Trossachs it caters for bus parties and is busy every night from early spring to Christmas and New Year, with several different coach parties rolling up its long drive from the lochside every afternoon. Behind the hotel, Glen Riabbach, which translated from the Gaelic means the Grizzly Valley, provides a two-hour circular route and, especially after heavy rainfall, the waterfalls on the Achray Water make an impressive site as they foam and froth their way down to the level of the loch.

Most famous of the walks is the climb up to the spur of Ben Venue, which affords a view second to none of Loch Katrine stretched out far below. The Victorian guidebook dictates that 'all who make this climb should carry with them a pocket edition of "The Lady of the Lake"' and it is still good advice, for this is exactly what Sir Walter Scott described his hero the bold Fitz-James enjoying in that famous poem, when he wrote:

> The broom's tough root a ladder made
> The hazel saplings lent their aid
> And thus an airy point he won
> Where, gleaming with the setting sun
> One burnish'd sheet of living gold
> Loch Katrine lay beneath him roll'd

The volcano-shaped Ben An is the dominant feature of the view from the Duke's Pass. (Arthur Down)

Today, unlike in old Fitz-James' time, it is possible to capture the whole scene not only in words but on film, and this is one shot guaranteed to wake up even the drowsiest of after-dinner guests when you show them your holiday slides or video.

This same Victorian guidebook describes Ben Venue as rising 'swell upon swell, alternately shaggy and sheer, a wilderness of huge boulders, pile upon pile, a heavenage of dark conglomerates'. Scott, again in 'The Lady of the Lake', is equally full of praise, writing:

High on the south, huge Ben Venue
Down on the Lake in masses threw
Crags, knolls, and mounds, confusedly hurl'd
The fragments of an earlier world

On the way up to Venue's 2,393ft-high summit, make an excuse to pause for breath and turn to admire its neighbour Ben An, which the old guidebook describes as:

a grey, weather-beaten, antediluvian-looking cone, which sternly frowns over the shaggy slopes and precipitous indentations, which in myriad form flanks the northern shore of the Katrine. Solitary and savage it seems a grim guardian mourning over the lost dominion of its solitude, and scowling defiance towards the arts which have hung highways upon his once pathless acclivities and bridged the blue waves, which lap its skirts, with the impetuous power of steam.

The latter comment, of course, relates to the introduction of paddle steamers on the loch. Nowadays Ben An also has to put up with hundreds of climbers swarming over its rocky crags as it is recognised as an excellent training ground for mountaineers.

Ben An is in the distance in this view taken in 1870. (Alistair Deayton)

For those keen on hill walking, instead of returning back down from the top of Ben Venue by the same route to the head of Loch Achray it is possible as an alternative to walk on down the other side to come out at Ledart Farm on the Aberfoyle to Inversnaid road. Do leave sufficient time, however, for this is about a five-hour hike and makes a satisfying whole day's outing.

Most visitors will explore the district crossed by the Duke's Pass by car or bus. Adding a bit of novelty is the opportunity to travel on the Trossachs Trundler, a veteran 1950s Bedford bus – like the one which disgorged the hockey-stick-wielding, gymslip-clad schoolgirls at the beginning of the famous *St Trinians* films – which plies between Callander and Aberfoyle by this scenic route.

A benefit, however, of travelling by private car is that it is then possible to enjoy at least a short walk by stopping at one of the lay-bys at the top of the road and getting out to climb to the nearby Trossachs Viewpoint. Many visitors also stop at this point on the Pass to have photographs taken with a piper who stations himself at this point in the hope of being repaid with lucrative tips for his patience.

From modern commercialism to times much, much more ancient; while walking up to the viewpoint notice how the layers of rocks have been meta-morphosed and turned upwards by an earthquake in geological times. Note too how springy is the peaty ground, which now barely covers the rocks.

At the viewpoint there is a direction-finder which indicates where Edinburgh and other cities and towns are situated. Nearby there is an excellent view across the valley to Brig O'Turk and the Glen Finglas Dam. This broad valley stretching out towards Loch Venachar and Callander is sometimes used by the RAF for low-flying exercises and it is strange to look down at their fighter jets swooping past, well below the level of the lookout.

The thick walls which make up the steep sides of the viewpoint are constructed of steel-grey slate and this is very appropriate, because it was this sturdy stone which gave the area its once-prosperous industry and the neighbouring quarries can be seen next on this route through the hills. Today the huge slate quarries lie deserted, but in Victorian times they were a hive of activity, as hundreds of men toiled day in day out to maintain the supplies of roofing slates needed for the tenement homes erected by the thousand during Glasgow's nineteenth-century housing boom. Although these were mainly working-class homes, they were solidly built of sandstone and roofed with slate. Now this would be expen-sive, but a century ago slate was an economic choice for roofing.

Probably the earliest written mention of the Aberfoyle slate quarries, which was recorded as early as 1724, comments 'excellent be sclait'. When the Earl of Menteith was asked to supply slates for the roofing of the buildings in Stirling Castle, it is believed that he had them quarried at Aberfoyle as this was the nearest source. By Victorian times the quarries had grown to become the third largest in Scotland, only Ballachulish in Argyllshire and Craiglea on the Earl of Mansfield's estate at Logiealmond 14 miles north-west of Perth being more productive.

A nineteenth-century account of the slate quarries states:

As well as the skill of the workers who blast the slate from the hillside towering above them, the expertise of those of their fellows, who then set upon the rocks thus dislodged and swiftly and accurately split them into the desired size of slates, must be admired. This art is learned from an early age and many of the speediest workers were mere boys. Four classes of slates are produced. They are described as, 'Duchess', 'Countess', 'Sizeable' and 'Undersized'. The first mentioned are the largest being 24 inches long by a foot broad, while the 'Countess' slates are twenty inches by ten inches. The other two classes are smaller. Each crew of workers makes all four sizes if the quality of the rock upon which they work allows this. Each man is paid by the thousand slates which he produces and different rates apply to the different sizes, giving a clear meaning to the term piecework. The men work in pairs, one splitting the slates and the other dressing them. Provided they are kept busy with a steady supply of good-quality rock each man can produce around one thousand slates a day.

At the entrance to the slate quarries on the Duke's Pass, the Quarry Master's House is now a holiday cottage. When the quarries were at their busiest in the middle of the nineteenth century, many of the workers lived on the site and there was a school for their children. (Arthur Down)

With such vast quantities of slates being produced, transport was of vital importance. Eventually, in the latter half of the nineteenth century, a narrow-gauge railway was built to carry them down to the railhead at Aberfoyle, which had been established specifically to transport the loads of slates to Glasgow. The track from the quarries came down the side of Craigmore and entered the village opposite the present church manse. There was a loading bank where Craigfoot Terrace is now situated. From there the laden bogies were pulled by Clydesdale horses to the station and, after the contents were loaded onto the waiting train, they returned them to the foot of the hill. There the empty bogies were hooked on to a continuous chain and the weight of the full hutches coming down pulled them up to the summit. From there they were hauled back by horses to be filled again at the quarries.

To begin with the Aberfoyle quarries were tenanted by individuals. In 1825 they were being worked by Duncan Macfarlane and in 1847 the tenant was Peter McKeich. In the 1850s there was a huge increase in demand for slates, because of the house-building boom in Glasgow and the lease of the quarries was taken over by a company. It was able to invest more capital in the development of the quarries and greatly increased the workforce. As a result of the remoteness of the site of the quarries from the village of Aberfoyle, many of the quarrymen brought their whole families to live up there in the hills and the new owners encouraged this by establishing a school and paying the salary of a schoolmaster. He must have been kept busy, because at one time the number of children on the role of the school at the quarry was greater than the total of boys and girls attending the school in Aberfoyle, whose Victorian grey whinstone buildings can still be seen on the road leading out to Loch Ard. Certainly the school at the quarry must have been the best supplied in the whole of Scotland with the slates on which nineteenth-century pupils did their writing and practised their sums.

At the quarry the only remaining building stands at the entrance just off the main road. This small whitewashed house was the home of the quarry manager. It has been restored and is now used as a holiday cottage. At one time the quarry company also owned the block of red sandstone buildings on the corner of Main Street and the foot of the Duke's Pass, and what is now the office of the local branch of the Bank of Scotland was at one time the home of one of the quarry officials.

In addition to the slate quarries there also used to be a whin quarry, which was developed by the then local government body, Perthshire County Council, when it took over responsibility from the former Road Commissioners for the development and repair of highways in the area and required material for road metal. Until this time, material for road repairs had simply been acquired by picking up stones from the roadside and transporting them by horse-drawn cart to the place where they were required. Once at the site, labourers had the hard job of smashing them up with picks and hammers to form the required road metal.

After the quarries, travelling towards Aberfoyle the road continues past the entrance to the Achray Forest Drive, which is dealt with in the next chapter. It then twists and turns its way, corkscrew-like, down to the entrance to the Forest Centre. The centre premises and the adjacent warden's house are fine examples of buildings constructed from local slate.

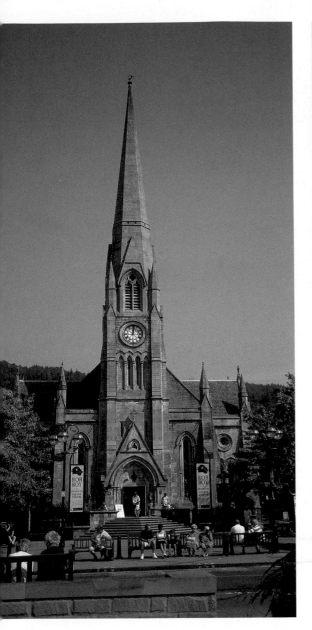

1 Ancaster Square, Callander, with the spire of the former St Kessog's kirk, now the Rob Roy Visitor Centre.

2 Dreadnought Hotel.

3 Ben Ledi looms over the river Teith.

4 Callander Main Street.

5 Kilmahog, with Ben Ledi in background.

6 Toll House, Kilmahog.

7 Loch Venachar.

8 Trossachs Kirk.

9, 10 Loch Achray.

11 Loch Achray.

12 Ben Venue and the Achray Hotel, formerly the Duke of
Montrose's hunting lodge.

13 Loch Achray.

14 Ben An.

15 Loch Achray and the Trossachs Hotel.

16 Loch Drunkie.

17 Aberfoyle Slate Quarries.

18 Entrance to the Achray Forest Drive.

19 Scottish Wool Experience.

20 Aberfoyle kirk with Doon Hill in the background.

21 Loch Ard.

22 Aberfoyle with Limecraig in the background.

Following pages

23 Loch Ard with Ben Lomond in the background.

24 Loch Ard.

25 Milton with millwheel.

chapter six

The Forest Park

The Queen Elizabeth Forest Park was inaugurated in 1953, the year of Her Majesty's Coronation. It is the largest forest not just in Scotland, but in the whole of Great Britain. The main body of the forest stretches uninterrupted from the east shore of Loch Lomond almost as far as Thornhill and Callander, with a long hooked arm reaching all the way north past Strathyre almost to Kingshouses on the road to Crianlarich. In total the area of the Forest Park is 9,000 square kilometres which takes in 50,000 acres, or 20,000 hectares, as the Forestry Commission now describes it. Approximately three quarters of its area is planted with trees. The rest is taken up with hill and mountain tops, rivers and lochs and the roads and paths which stretch out through the Forest Park, rather like the roots of one of its trees.

Aforestation in Scotland has been a controversial subject ever since some of the earliest plantings in this enormous forest took place, when the first of the lands which it covers were purchased in 1928. Acquisition of more and more acres, mainly from large landowners such as Montrose Estates, continued until 1951, shortly before the creation of the Forest Park.

Many opponents of the development of commercial forestry on this huge scale consider that the hillsides should be left starkly and dramatically bare, while the foresters on the other hand have tried over the decades to raise the tree line ever higher and to clad the slopes in green. Indeed they have been so successful that the spread of the trees can best be likened to the science fiction novel *The Day of the Triffids*, and over half of the United Kingdom's forestry industry is now based in Scotland. In recognition of this, the government department responsible both for managing all state-run forests and for advising the owners of private woodlands about official policy, the Forestry Commission, has its headquarters at Corstorphine in Edinburgh, where it occupies the distinctive modern, smoked-glass-fronted building opposite the zoo.

Apart from its obvious aim to produce timber, the Forestry Commission is charged with wildlife conservation and with looking after and promoting the amenities of the woodlands under its protection. This latter objective involves providing information about them to the public and nowhere does it do so better than at the Forest Centre, perched dramatically on the hillside above Aberfoyle.

Glimpsed from afar the Forest Centre with its pillared exterior looks somewhat like a Greek temple, but within its light and airy interior it is truly the wonders of nature which are worshipped. The centre was first opened in 1962, when it was presented to the Forestry Commission by the Carnegie (United Kingdom) Trust, which administers the rich legacy left to the nation by Scotland's greatest benefactor, Dunfermline-born steel magnate Andrew Carnegie. To begin with the centre was called the David Marshall Lodge, in honour of the chairman of the Carnegie Trust, and was run on an entirely non-commercial basis, providing free picnicking facilities both indoors and outside for visitors, and toilets and washing facilities for hill walkers. The centrepiece was a wonderfully detailed three-dimensional model of the whole of the Trossachs.

Since then it has been extended and its excellent facilities include a small audio-visual theatre, a popular café restaurant, a forest shop selling high-quality products related to the area and several small workshops, where local craftsmen ranging from a resident woodcarver to potters, painters and weavers can demonstrate their skills and offer their products for sale. Mountain bikes are also available for hire through a franchise operated by a local company.

Around the centre well-designed, detailed displays help visitors gain a good impression of the work and life of the forest. Take time to browse through them and you'll discover that most of the timber produced and sold within the Aberfoyle Forest Area is softwood from coniferous, cone-bearing trees such as spruce, larch, pine and various fir trees, about twelve important species in all. Some, like the larch and the spruce, are very easily identified. The larch is the one which turns brown in colour in winter as it is the only deciduous conifer in the park. To learn this simply remember 'larch loses leaves', although strictly speaking it is its needles which it casts. The greenery of the spruce on the other hand retains a silvery sheen all year round. The predominant tree in the west of the Queen Elizabeth Forest Park is the Sitka spruce, while the Scots pine holds sway further east. Other conifers grown in the Forest Park include Norway spruce, European and Japanese larch, Douglas fir, Silver fir and lodgepole pine. The latter takes its unusual name from the fact that in its native United States and Canada it is said to have been grown to provide the centre pole for the tepees and wigwams of the native Indian populations. The timber produced from the lodgepole pine is similar to that obtained from our native Scots pine, but the transatlantic import will grow in much poorer conditions. Indeed it is claimed that lodgepoles can be grown on the poorest soil and the most exposed of sites, where not even the hardiest breeds of sheep will survive, high on the slopes of the hillsides.

Trees are, of course, grown to make money, and to obtain this they have sooner or later to be felled, but while this is inevitable it is also very carefully

The Queen Elizabeth Forest Park, founded in Her Majesty's Coronation Year 1953, is the largest wooded area in the whole of Britain. (Arthur Down)

managed to cause as little hurt to the eye as possible. This is done by following carefully designed landscape plans to decide which of the 400 to 600 hectares (1,000 to 1,500 acres) of forest to fell each year to reach the target of producing 270,000 tonnes of timber. 40,000 tonnes of this comes from thinnings whose removal opens up the younger trees and enables them in the long run to produce bigger and better logs. Output is expected to reach 291,000 tonnes in the millennium and it is important that visitors should remember that forestry is similar to farming in that it is essential that it makes profits and that the trees they see around them are its cash crop.

The majority of the trees which are felled, amounting to about 70 per cent, are harvested with their branches cut off and cut into set lengths, before being extracted from the forest by machine, unlike times past when horses were used to pull them down to the forest tracks. Nowadays one machine can cut the same amount as twenty men with saws and it never complains about having to work on even the coldest, wettest and bleakest of days, when sleet scuds in from over the shoulder of Ben Lomond obliterating the view and making it feel so cold that no sensible soul would choose to be out on the hillside.

The remaining 30 per cent of the trees on the steeper slopes do however still require to be manually felled, hopefully when the weather in the Trossachs is a shade better. These trees are then extracted using a cablecrane winch.

A large proportion of the timber from the Queen Elizabeth Forest Park goes to sawmills, where it is cut into wood suitable for house building and other constructional uses. The lower-grade logs are made into fencing materials and also into boards needed to make the ubiquitous wooden pallets without which warehouses could not operate and forklift trucks would grind to a halt.

Small thinnings and other smaller-diameter logs, known as roundwood, are sold mainly to Caberboard, in whose factory near Stirling it is turned into

Forestry lorries in their yard below Limecraig at Aberfoyle. (William F. Hendrie)

particle board, while the remainder goes mostly to the Caledonian Mill at Irvine to be converted into wood pulp for the production of paper. For many people in Scotland, the timber framework used in the construction of their modern homes, their house's chipboard floors and their fitted kitchen and bathroom cupboards have probably originated in the Queen Elizabeth Forest Park, as well, of course, as the newspapers and magazines that they read, once they have moved in.

The felled areas of the Forest Park are replanted usually within two years and for conservation reasons have a quarter of their open space dedicated to the growing of native Scottish broadleaved trees such as oak, birch, alder, willow and the rowan or mountain ash. Visitors particularly love the latter as their bright orange berries give such a splash of autumn colour, before the birds devour them eagerly, as welcome winter fodder. A very old Scottish tradition also claims that planting a rowan is guaranteed to keep the witches away.

The Queen Elizabeth Forest Park is very carefully managed using a set of complex design plans. Using these plans, felling and planting areas are shaped, sometimes quite intricately, to harmonise with the natural form of the land, its hills and hollows and importantly its streams and lochs. Clear felling of whole areas means that when the time comes to re-stock them the opportunity can be taken to introduce a wider variety of species than was possible in the early pioneering years of forestry development. This policy has helped to remove some of the earlier objections from nature lovers who complained bitterly that the spread of the forest created deep dark canyons between the rows of conifers, where the sun never penetrated and undergrowth could not flourish so that they were very inhospitable places for wildlife. Now skilful planting following the detailed design plans means that it is possible, for instance, to create dappled shade along the banks of streams and this favours water life. Likewise human visitors are given similar consideration by ensuring that picnic places and forest walks are designed to give pleasant surroundings and interesting views, while disturbance of sensitive wildlife is always avoided.

As a result of the rich variety of structure, soils and resultant vegetation brought about by the great land upheavals of the Highland Boundary Fault, there are many Sites of Special Scientific Interest (SSSI) in the Forest Park and these are managed by the Forestry Commission in close conjunction with Scottish Natural Heritage with whom it has an excellent working relationship. In total twenty-five SSSIs are under Forestry Commission ownership.

There are about 2,671 hectares of broadleaved woodland in the district, much of it within the Queen Elizabeth Forest Park. The area of native broadleaved woodland is being increased every year as part of routine forest design planning with broadleaved trees comprising not less than 5 per cent of all replanting. In addition and as part of the Ben Lomond National Memorial Park, a joint venture between the Forestry Commission and the National Trust for Scotland, the entire coniferous woodland comprising about 1,000 hectares on the east shore of Loch Lomond is being converted to native woodland.

Another forward-looking policy being implemented in the Queen Elizabeth Forest Park is the identification of sheltered areas, where conifers can be retained until they reach their biological maturity, which means that in the future some of the trees being planted now will be allowed to grow until they are over 150 years old. Such long-term retentions will no doubt prove of great ecological interest to future foresters and a truly big attraction for visitors in centuries to come.

Even at present some of the softwood trees in the Aberfoyle area are of considerable age, as some of the plantings in the Forest Park date back to 1930. Even older are some of the hardwood trees, especially the sessile oaks, which are descendants of the old oak coppices established on a commercial basis by the Montrose Estates, as the bark from these trees was the source of tannin required by the Scottish leather-making industry. A typical oak coppice has been recreated in the Forest Park within easy walking distance of the Forest Centre on the hillside behind Aberfoyle and it gives an insight into the way that such woodlands were managed by the Duke of Montrose's foresters since the early seventeenth century.

Nowadays, in contrast to these ancient methods, the most modern approaches are adopted in the management of the Forest Park. Wherever possible the ground within it is cultivated with excavator moulding, this being the preferred method to give the trees the best possible start. Conifers and broadleaf species, primarily for conservation, landscaping and amenity purposes, are planted at 1,100 trees to each hectare and the young trees are carefully protected from damage by the red and roe deer and rabbits which also have the forest as their home. In addition they have to be kept safe from insects and weeds, but the greatest danger in the forest is always from fire. The fire risk is particularly great because two million people live within the forest district and four million of Scotland's five million population live within a 50-mile radius of the main forest centres. Fire breaks, the clearings seen between the belts of trees, are deliberately created to help stop the spread of any outbreak. Prevention is, however, better than cure and strict precautions are introduced during dry spells and other high-risk periods. In the past there were four fire lookout towers in the area around Aberfoyle and the tower of the Forest Centre was also designed for this purpose. From these hilltop lookouts watchers had to use hand-cranked field telephones and landlines to inform the forestry head-quarters of any suspected outbreak. Nowadays the most modern means of communication have replaced these old methods, save vital minutes and help reduce the danger.

If a fire does catch hold, however, it is still the same old back-breaking work to extinguish it and stacks of fire-beaters can be seen at intervals through the forest. Originally their bunches of birch twigs bound to long wooden poles looked like witches' broomsticks, but now most are equipped with more effi-cient rubber paddles at the firefighting end. Visitors can help greatly to prevent outbreaks by not lighting campfires or barbecues in the forest, apart from at approved picnic sites, and never throwing away cigarette ends.

The fact that the Queen Elizabeth Forest Park is so easily within reach of all those who live in Central Scotland means that the Forestry Commission gives particular consideration to the careful maximisation of its great recreational potential. Non-commercial facilities include the Forest Centre, the Achray Forest Drive, thirty-five car parks, ten youth campsites, thirty walks plus a hundred kilometres of trails, thirty picnic places, ten wayfaring courses and twenty cycle trails. In addition, speciality recreational activities include the popular Swedish sport of orienteering, which is like a car rally on foot, horse riding, pony trekking, archery, mountain bike races, deer stalking, fishing, car rallies and even husky dog training. Some visitors are concerned that Forest Enterprise permits controlled hunting, but it is to the benefit of the remaining deer that culling takes place when their numbers grow too large and the shoot is always directed by highly experienced stalkers.

On the commercial recreational front the Forestry Commission manages seventeen holiday cabins, built, of course, with logs chopped straight from the forest and constructed by the park's own workers. It also operates two campsites, beautifully situated on the east shore of Loch Lomond and on the banks of the river Forth at Cobbleland on the outskirts of Aberfoyle. Together these well-run sites provide around 300 pitches. Eighty of the pitches are let to caravan owners for the season, while the remainder of the spaces are available for touring cara-vans and campers. These sites are operated by Forest Enterprise Holidays, a specialist business unit which is part of the Forestry Commission. Details of avail-ability and prices may be obtained from Forest Enterprise at its modern offices at the entrance to Aberfoyle, telephone 01877 382383 or by faxing 01877 382694. The postcode for the offices is FK8 3UX. Do use the code, as letters addressed simply to Aberfoyle have a horrible habit of being sent first to Wales and only after failing to find any such 'Aber' are redirected back to Scotland.

From these offices at Aberfoyle, the estate management, civil engineering and mechanical aspects of the Queen Elizabeth Forest Park are also managed, including 400 hectares of agricultural leases and grazing land and over 600 kilometres of forest roads. Next to the offices are the garages and repair workshops for the Forest Park's fleet of vehicles, which range from cars and minibuses to huge timber processors and excavator harvesters. The latter look particularly enormous when encountered on the narrow roads within the forest, which for safety reasons are strictly out of bounds to private motorists.

The one exception is the Achray Forest Drive. Opened in 1977 to mark the Silver Jubilee of Her Majesty Queen Elizabeth, it permits drivers access to explore 7½ miles of winding forest roads and is open from April until October. A one-way system is operated, starting from the quarries on the Duke's Pass. At the beginning of the drive is a car park, where an information board gives up-to-date information. First of the attractions of this exciting winding drive comes almost at the beginning when, round the second bend, little-known Lochan Reoidhte comes into sight. Shaped like a footprint, its name is pronounced locally as 'Loch Roach'. On the wooded hillside opposite the far end of the loch is an old quarry.

Achray Forest Drive in spring truly offers every shade of green, while in autumn it rivals the woodlands of New England with its rich tapestry of warm reds, russets, gold and orange, but no matter when during the season you drive through it, there is always something different to see. After a tight U-bend the track twists north, then south again, before a long comparatively straight stretch leads east through the depths of the forest to emerge at the first of the viewpoints overlooking Loch Drunkie. Just over half a mile further round the coast there is a second viewpoint, which looks out over the whole body of the loch. The forest drive then hugs the shore of the loch until it turns round its western end and afterwards reaches the major development along its length, a visitor centre, with car parking, toilets and playground for children. This is the halfway point on the drive.

From here the road leaves the lochside and continues inland through the forest, but those wishing to see more of Drunkie can do so by leaving the car in the parking ground and taking the clearly way-marked Pine Ridge Walk, which hugs its north shore for three quarters of a mile. At the far end of Pine Ridge Walk it rejoins the road. This gives the option of either completing the circle back to the car park at the visitor centre by the road or of turning back and again enjoying the stroll in the other direction beside the waters of the loch. Either way keep quiet and you may be rewarded with a glimpse of some of the creatures for whom the forest is their home, such as squirrels and rabbits. There are also larger mammals including red deer and the smaller Bambi-like roes as well as foxes and badgers, but they are shy and are seldom seen by day, most visitors having to be content to spot evidence of their presence from their tracks.

There is more chance of spotting birds along the drive, from mallard duck, coots and waterhens on the loch, to woodpeckers and treecreepers in the forest, but again visitors are unlikely to be fortunate enough to see the largest bird which frequents the Trossachs, the famous capercaillie. As large as a turkey, the big black-feathered male capercaillie has a fierce reputation and has been known to fly at and attack people blocking its path through the forest. It is indeed so formidable that its Gaelic name translates as the 'horse of the forest'.

In the early 1990s, however, a female capercaillie became almost domesticated. She took up residence in the forest, just behind Aberfoyle, and for several weeks paid daily visits to the grounds of Dounans Residential Outdoor Education Centre. There she appeared to thoroughly enjoy being petted and fed and having her brown feathers stroked by the pupils. When she had had enough attention she flew up onto the roof of the dormitory block overlooking the main camp square, then when hungry flew back across the grass to take up position at the dining hall steps, where titbits were most plentiful. For her own safety rather than that of the boys and girls, she was trapped several times and transported miles into the depths of the forest, but on every occasion she soon came back to the camp.

The exploits of the children-loving capercaillie featured in the pages of the *Sunday Post* and expert ornithologists suggested all kinds of theories as to why this normally reclusive bird had suddenly decided to seek human company. They included the possibility that she may have survived being shot and was as a result suffering from lead poisoning from the pellets lodged in her body! In the end the people-loving capercaillie was given her wish to stay amongst humans by being donated to Scotland's Safari and Leisure Park on the southern edge of the Trossachs at Blair Drummond.

It is interesting that while Scotland's Safari Park has done so much to interest visitors to the Trossachs in its collection of elephants, rhinos, giraffes, zebras, lions, tigers, bears, monkeys, ostriches, penguins, camels, llamas, antelopes, bison, wallabies and even meerkats, in contrast very little appears to have been done to ensure the future of Scotland's native capercaillie. In truth, the capercaillie did in fact die out in Scotland towards the end of the eighteenth century, when the last bird of the species was reported as having been shot in Aberdeenshire in 1785. It was not re-introduced until the first year of Queen Victoria's reign in 1837, when the Marquis of Breadalbane brought fifty of the birds from Sweden and released them as game birds on his estate in Perthshire. The capercaillies adapted successfully to life in the Highlands and soon also re-established themselves in the Trossachs. The whole idea in Victorian times was to provide Scotland with its largest and undoubtedly fiercest game bird, which would face up to any hunter and thus become all the more valued as a prize, although its forest diet of pine needles and the shoots of the young pine trees made its flesh so tainted with resin that it was completely inedible. Today the Trossachs is again one of the last places in Scotland where capercaillies can be found, although as their habitats have become increasingly threatened, they are now rare.

Another comparative rarity in the Trossachs is Great Britain's only poisonous snake. Little adders are found in the Queen Elizabeth Forest Park, but they do not pose any great threat to visitors as they are seldom seen and if they are spotted in the open they usually quickly slither away. Occasionally during hot weather visitors are lucky enough to see an adder, or viper as they are sometimes known, lying basking in the warmth of the sun. In this case the advice is to observe from a discreet distance before passing on by. Do not on any account poke an adder with a stick in an attempt to see it move, or in any other way disturb it.

There are also slow-worms in the area around Aberfoyle. Slow-worms are, however, not snakes. Unlike adders, slow-worms are non-poisonous and are completely harmless. Slow-worms are similar in size to adders but lack the latter's V-shape brownish markings down the back. If, however, you are close enough to distinguish this difference you are probably too close for comfort and should move clear.

If you are unfortunate enough to be bitten by an adder, the incident should be treated seriously and medical attention sought. Provided the correct treatment is administered there is little danger, but in the past decade one child has died as a result of an adder bite received while on a day outing to Aberfoyle because unfortunately his family did not take him to hospital until they returned to Glasgow, by which time it was too late for the usually foolproof antidote to take effect.

Back on the Achray Forest Drive the road continues in a north-westerly direction with trees on the left and Blackwater Marsh on the right. Down across the Black Water stream can be glimpsed Loch Venachar, into which it feeds. The Black Water flows out of Loch Achray and the Forest Drive descends onto the beautiful banks of that loch, following its south shore for over a mile. There are two parking spots along this stretch of the route and near the second of them is one of the sites where the Forestry Commission allows recognised youth organisations to pitch tents and camp. There can be few more scenic campsites in Scotland than this one with its view straight out across the waters of Loch Achray to the north shore, where the little Trossachs Kirk is situated directly opposite.

After leaving the side of Loch Achray the Forest Drive is almost at an end and a further three quarters of a mile brings drivers back to the busy traffic of the Duke's Pass. At this point there is the option of either turning right to drive down to the Trossachs Pier and back to Callander, or to head left and return past the quarries and back to the Forest Centre.

One feature of the Forest Centre which the Forestry Commission has not yet developed as a visitor attraction, is what lies deep in the hillside, directly below the building. It is, however, down there that the secret of the Forest Centre lies buried. Back in the 1960s, during the cold war, the centre was built as a clever disguise for a nuclear fallout shelter, in case the Russians ever launched their deadly missiles. The safety of its air-conditioned quarters was not provided, however, for the parents and children of Aberfoyle, but for the area's top local government officials and a few emergency service workers who might be needed to man the radios and telephone exchange to keep in touch with whatever remained of the outside world after the detonation of a nuclear bomb. Bunk beds and plastic water containers, hopefully never to be needed, still lie waiting in readiness in the Aberfoyle Emergency Regional Fallout Centre, which is a much smaller-scale version of the one between Anstruther and St Andrews in Fife to which the Secretary of State for Scotland was to scurry and which, although his apartments are still kept strictly private, has now been opened to curious visitors as the attraction known as the Secret Bunker. While there are no plans in the immediate future to open the Aberfoyle nuclear shelter to the public, observant visitors can still spot where the heavy steel shutters were to be hurriedly placed over the ground-floor windows and, out in the grounds of the Forest Centre, the hidden surface outlets for the underground air purification system can still be seen.

The Forest Centre, which is open daily from Easter to October and then during afternoons, weather permitting, through until Christmas, provides information, leaflets and maps which describe the extensive system of clearly way-marked and signposted walks and bicycle trails, which like the roots of one of its trees seem to reach out to every part of the forest. Like Boots the Chemist, the Queen Elizabeth Forest Park does indeed 'have branches everywhere!' One of the most interesting of these easily walked routes, which starts right from the front door of the centre, is the Highland Boundary Fault Trail. Illustrated, interpretive stations at regular intervals along its route explain in a concise, clear and yet amusing manner how this upheaval took place and the consequences of it on the present-day geography of the Trossachs. In total the Highland Boundary Fault Trail is 4 miles long and needs about two hours to complete, but it is possible to tackle shorter sections by following the parts nearest to the Forest Centre on successive visits.

For those who prefer a shorter stroll, the walk from the Forest Centre to the Waterfall of the Little Fawn is a very good choice. On the way down to it, pause by the little lochan in the grounds of the centre and, if you visit it in the spring, spot the myriad host of tadpoles which swarm in its shallow waters, before turning 'Beauty and the Beast'-like into wee green puddocks. By the look of things, there must surely be enough tadpoles in this one wee lochan to supply a mandatory jam jar full of them to every primary school classroom in the whole of Scotland.

After watching the frogs, the tadpoles from which they grew and also other fish in the man-made lochan, continue on down the hillside path and listen out for the sound of the waterfall before you see it. Its rumbling roar gets louder, then, rounding a wooded corner, it appears suddenly, as if by magic, plummeting 55ft straight down onto the rocks below. Why it is called the Waterfall of the Little Fawn is a mystery lost in the mists of its crashing waters, but it is fun to make up stories about the little baby deer from which it takes its name. Sometimes those who are entranced by the sparkle of its dancing waters suggest other names which they feel better describe the waterfall and the enchanted spot which its constantly flowing water has through the centuries etched in this part of the forest. These falls are also known locally as the Gray Mare's Tail, which is, of course, also the name of a much larger waterfall near Moffat in the Southern Uplands named after the horse on which Tam O'Shanter succeeded in out-running Cutty Sark and her fellow witches in Robert Burns' poem.

While there is no guarantee of spotting any witches, the area around the foot of the Waterfall of the Little Fawn is a very good place for birdwatching as it is a habitat much favoured by little black and white pied wagtails. These attractive little birds, which always seem to dart about in such a hurry that they seem to be on roller skates, used to be called water wagtails, a description which appeared to encapsulate why they are so plentiful in this sheltered setting at the foot of the falls. In contrast to the black and white plumage of the wee wagtails, the chaffinches which also frequent this area add a splash of colour as the males with their pink breasts and pale blue bonnets out-dazzle the dowdier green-brown feathers of the females. The cocky, almost pugnacious male chaffinches even announce their bright colours, with their cry of 'Pink, pink'. Listen out too for the colourful little yellowhammers, with their distinctive call of 'a little bit of bread and no cheese'.

The yellow hammers love nesting in gorse and so are well catered for on the hillside above Aberfoyle, as it is turned into a blaze of colour by this prickly bush in the spring and early months of the summer. In marked contrast to the exceedingly prickly nature of the golden gorse, there are also patches of yellow broom. Its slender branches of long, smooth, green leaves did indeed used to be pulled and gathered in past centuries to provide brooms and brushes for domestic use. The broom is also still sometimes referred to by the old Scottish term of 'whin'.

When each year the hillside on the edge of the Forest Park above Aberfoyle is gilded by the blossoming of the gorse and the broom, another bird cry often heard in the territory between the falls and Dounans Residential Outdoor Education Centre in the month of May is the distinctive one of the cuckoo, as many of these rogues of the bird world nest in the area. The grey-feathered, speckle-breasted female cuckoo lays or deposits with her beak one of her eggs in the nests of other birds, particularly preferring as foster parents the pied wagtails. Before flying off she then ejects most or all of the chosen foster parents' own eggs. Thus nature ensures that the cuckoo's own demanding offspring will receive all the attention and food which it requires as it grows into a brown-plumaged, speckle-breasted chick, much larger than its unfortunate foster parents!

Although the cuckoo is doing simply as nature intended and birds and beasts should not be judged by human standards of behaviour, its unfortunate habits have never endeared it to birdwatching enthusiasts. On the other hand, bird-watchers love to spot a song thrush (or mavis as they are still known in Scotland), but unfortunately in the Trossachs, as elsewhere in the country, they are becoming increasingly rare, as are blackbirds and even sparrows, while the more belligerent starlings rule the roost along with crows and scavenging magpies.

The edge of the Forest Park is also a good area to spot birds of prey. Kestrels are common and sparrowhawks can be spotted, but the most impressive sight is to see buzzards wheeling high in the air over Limecraig.

From Dounans Residential Outdoor Education Centre pupils often come up to the Waterfall of the Little Fawn to take part in bird-spotting by day or bat-watching by night or simply to indulge in the delights of paddling amongst the rocks at the foot of the falls, but also to enjoy playing their home-made instruments to create improvised music with the water's rushing roar as their backing tape. On warm summer days, when the glade at the foot of the water-fall is a veritable sun trap, one may be inspired to imagine that the Waterfall of the Little Fawn is situated not in Scotland, but far away on a south sea island paradise, while on colder days the youngsters' thoughts may well turn to a theme inspired by the native Indian tribes of North America, as they beat out a rhythm on their handmade tom-toms to the accompaniment of recorders or simple flutes made in the camp craft room.

The walk to the Waterfall of the Little Fawn need, however, not only be a treat for the young. There is a rustic wooden handrail along all of the sloping sections of the Waterfall Trail, which makes it possible for even the less physically able to enjoy discovering its delights. A forest park is obviously not the easiest of places to provide facilities for handicapped visitors. The Forestry Commission is, however, clearly conscious of its duties to them and, although it does not meet all of the standards required to be officially classified as offering full access to the physically challenged, it has tried to cater for them in many ways, from providing ramped access to the visitor centre, to providing disabled toilets there and at the Loch Lomond and Cobbleland campsites, to ensuring that the picnic tables are accessible to those with wheelchairs, to making certain that the door-ways in the log cabins on Loch Lubnaig are wide enough to allow those in wheelchairs to enjoy holidays in them.

To try to make its facilities as widely available to all visitors as possible, the Forestry Commission also offers a ranger service and these enthusiastic members of staff organise a wide range of activities, from guided walks to fungi forays, illustrated talks and birdwatching expeditions. The Commission is also always looking to the future and is currently co-operating with the National Trust for Scotland to develop the Ben Lomond National Memorial Park, which the Secretary of State for Scotland opened in 1997 as a fitting tribute to those who fought and in some cases died serving their country in the wars of the twentieth century. Between them the two organisations own and manage the Memorial Park in equal parts, ensuring that these lands on the eastern shore of Loch Lomond and the slopes of the ben will always remain accessible to visi-tors.

Within the Memorial Park, Forest Enterprise is undertaking what it describes as 'possibly one of the biggest operations of its kind in the world to restore the Atlantic Oakwoods'. This work will lead to major improvements to nationally important wildlife habitats and to the surrounding landscape, and will open up opportunities for the phased introduction of new walks, trails and facilities, well into the new millennium.

chapter seven

Aberfoyle, the Magical Kingdom

Aberfoyle, the busy southern entrance to the Trossachs, has not always been where it stands today. The original village was situated about 1 mile to the south on the opposite side of the river Forth. There at Kirkton of Aberfoyle, the church from which it took its name and the minister's home, the manse, still stand.

The ruins of the kirk remain and the kirkyard which surrounds it attracts many visitors, as it is here that the tombstone of its most celebrated minister, the Revd Robert Kirk, is to be found; however, whether his skeleton lies beneath it has always been a matter of dispute. Shortly after he had moved to Aberfoyle from Balquhidder, where he had led a douce and respectable life throughout the whole of his preaching career, in 1686 Revd Kirk suddenly announced that he could communicate with the fairies and, as a result of his threatening to reveal their secrets, they are said to have spirited his body away!

For Robert Kirk, being called to Aberfoyle to succeed his father must have seemed like coming home, as it was in the town's old manse that he had been born in 1640. Significantly, he was the seventh son of the parish minister, but throughout his childhood he showed no sign of having been gifted with second sight, which according to Scottish folklore such a child may be expected to possess. Instead he enjoyed a very normal boyhood, his father managing to scrape together from his stipend the fees to send him as a boarder to the High School of Dundee, which was at the time reckoned to be one of the finest schools in Scotland. Young Kirk was an able pupil and went on to study at Edinburgh University, from where he graduated in 1661 with a Master of Arts degree at the age of only seventeen.

The presbytery of Dunblane were sufficiently impressed with his academic prowess to grant him a bursary to go on to study theology at the University of St Andrews, where he later gained his Doctor of Divinity degree. Thereafter, as mentioned in chapter two, he was called to become minister of Balquhidder.

Robert Kirk might indeed have spent the whole of his ministry at Balquhidder had it not been for the death of his wife in 1680. He later remarried and this

Thatched Highland cottages at
Kirkton of Aberfoyle, c.1900.
(J. & C. McCutcheon)

time he took as his wife the daughter of Campbell of Fordy. She made a good
mother to the two children of his first marriage and soon added to the Kirk
family by bearing him a son. Around the same time the parish of Aberfoyle fell
vacant in 1685 and, after twenty-one years at Balquhidder and perhaps to mark
a new start for his family, at the age of forty-four Revd Kirk applied to become
its minister. With his local connections as the son of the manse and his impressive record of theological scholarship at Balquhidder, it was not surprising that
he was successful in his bid and the parishioners were delighted to welcome
him as minister.

Soon after, on 9 June 1685, the family left Balquhidder and settled into the
manse at Kirkton of Aberfoyle. However, a strange change then came over
Robert Kirk. Instead of devoting his time to pastoral visits to his parishioners, he
took to walking away from their homes to spend many hours exploring nearby
Doon Hill, whose rounded slopes overlook the manse.

Local tradition has it that the rounded summit of Doon Hill was the site of a
fort belonging to one of the early Scots kings of Dalriada. Mr D.S. McNair,
District Forest Officer at Aberfoyle in the 1960s, wrote that: 'The hill would
certainly provide a strong defensive position, lying as it does, in a loop of the
river Forth, with swampy ground at its base. It would control the route of anyone
attempting to travel up the valley to Loch Ard and beyond.'

Translated from the Gaelic Doon Hill means Fairy Hill, and as a lad young
Robert Kirk had often played there with his brothers, sisters and friends, perhaps
imagining they were the advancing troops of old and certainly enjoying
climbing its trees, playing hide and seek and finding its thickly wooded slopes
the ideal setting for all kinds of imaginary adventures.

Now, however, as a mature, staid adult he always went alone and usually in
the dead of night. No longer did he joke or jest – as he had no doubt often done
with his boyhood friends – about the fairies from whom the hill took its name,
because now he became convinced that not only were the wee folk real, but
that he could speak to them and that they had chosen him to interpret their
thoughts to the outside world.

To get as close as possible to the elven inhabitants of Doon Hill, Kirk took to lying down on the hillside and pressing his ear to its leaf-covered surface. Sometimes he stayed away from the manse all night, to the alarm of his family, and would only reluctantly return as dawn broke, when his wife went to fetch him.

By 1690, Kirk decided that his nocturnal wanderings had resulted in sufficient information from the little people to allow him to begin writing a weird and wonderful manuscript, which he entitled *The Secret Commonwealth of the Elves, Fauns and Fairies*. In a perfectly matter-of-fact way he described the inhabitants of Doon Hill as 'The People of Peace' or 'The Good People' and explained that he could understand them as they spoke the same language as those ordinary mortals who lived above ground. The wee folk of Doon Hill, however, chose to say little, he stated, preferring to communicate with each other through a system of whistling, which he described as 'clear not rough'.

In *The Secret Commonwealth*, the minister then went on to describe the appearance of the elves, fauns and fairies, explaining that:

> their bodies be so pliable through the subillity of the spirits that agitate them, that they can make them appear or disappear at pleasure. Some have bodies so spungious, thin and desecat, that they are fed by only sucking into some fine spirituous liquors that pierce like pure air and oil. Others feed more gross on the substance of corns and liquors that grow on the surface of the earth, which these fairies steal away, partly invisible, partly preying on the grain, as do the crows and the mice. They are sometimes heard to bake bread, strike hammers and do such-like services within the little hillocks they most haunt.

When they chose to be visible to the human eye, he claimed that they 'are seen to wear plaids and variegated garments as worn in the Highlands of Scotland'.

Moving on to describe the habits and lifestyle of the fairies, Mr Kirk confessed that they could sometimes be mischievous, stealing milk from the cows and damaging the local farmers' crops. More seriously, he alleged that they sometimes stole the unborn babies of pregnant women or even spirited away newborn infants. Such kidnaps could, however, be prevented if during confinements a piece of cold iron was placed in the bed of the expectant mother. Kirk explained that all fairies feared iron because the great northern iron mines lay adjacent to the place of eternal punishment and 'have a savour odious to these fascinating creatures.'

'Fascinating creatures' or not, the wee folk appear to have resented the revelation of such secrets by the minister, for one bright moonlit night in May 1692, as he walked alone as usual to the summit of Doon Hill, clad only in his long white nightshirt, they are alleged to have spirited his soul away, leaving only his body on its cold slopes. There it was discovered next morning and those who found it described it as though the minister had died from 'a fit of apoplexy'.

Three days later, as was the Scottish custom, the minister's funeral took place. It was a particularly sad occasion because Kirk's wife was expecting another child.

To make matters even worse, those in the know amongst the mourners whispered that the minister's mortal remains were not in the wooden coffin, which was laid to rest in the grave beside the old church at Aberfoyle, because the fairies had spirited his body away during the time of mourning and that it had been replaced by 'a rickle of stanes' to maintain appearances by weighing it down.

These sacrilegious suspicions appeared justified when, a few days later, the minister's cousin shocked the entire neighbourhood by reporting that Kirk had materialised before him and told him to inform their relative, the local laird Graham of Duchray, that he was not dead but had simply fallen into a swoon, during which the fairies had carried him off into their world beneath Doon Hill. When he went to Duchray Castle in the forest in Strathard he was to inform Graham that Kirk had promised to reappear soon after his wife gave birth to their child and that this would take place on the day of the new baby's baptism. In addition he was told to stress to Graham that he should come to the christening armed with a knife, which at the moment of Kirk's reappearance he was to be ready to throw over the minister's head, because, as he had reported in *The Secret Commonwealth*, the fairies were terrified of iron. The throwing of the knife would therefore break their spell and Kirk declared that he would thereupon return to life.

At first, although he told his neighbours, the cousin hesitated about delivering such a strange and fanciful message to such an important person as Graham of Duchray. Angry at his cousin's disobedience, Kirk reappeared before him again and threatened to disturb his sleep every single night without fail until Graham of Duchray was given his instructions.

Next morning the cousin did as he was ordered and went to Duchray Castle to tell the sceptical laird the news. Days later Kirk's wife gave birth to their baby and, despite his doubts, Graham of Duchray did arrive for the baptism, carrying a knife. As was common in Scotland at this time, the baptism took place not in the church but in the drawing room of the manse, which was packed with relatives, friends and parishioners, who crowded in for the occasion no doubt because they were more than a little curious to see for themselves whether Kirk would indeed come back to life.

The baptism service took its usual uneventful course. The baby, in its long, white, lace christening gown, was handed to the minister, who anointed its head with the holy water, pronounced its name and returned it safely to its mother's arms. Then suddenly, as the ceremony ended, the apparently very solid figure of the Revd Kirk strode through the drawing room door!

What happened next was recorded by Kirk's successor at Aberfoyle, the Revd Robert Graham. He reported that Graham of Duchray was completely stunned by Kirk's reappearance, so much so that he forgot to hurl the knife. Kirk stared straight at the laird, but he failed to react. In total shocked silence, Kirk gave him a reproachful look and, when he still did not fling the knife, walked on past him and left the room by the other door, never to be seen again.

Kirk's wife and family had no doubt what had happened to him. His eldest son Colin, who was a successful lawyer in Edinburgh, wrote: 'He has gone to his own kind.' When his mother died the manuscript of his father's *Secret Commonwealth* passed to him. Thereafter for a time it was lost, but was rediscovered in 1815 by Sir Walter Scott. Scott was so intrigued with what he read that when he came to the Trossachs he made his headquarters at the old manse at Aberfoyle, where this unusual book had been written.

The original version of Kirk's *Secret Commonwealth* is now preserved in the library of the University of Edinburgh in George Square. It is a remarkable text to have been written in the seventeenth century, especially when it is remembered that it is the work of a minister, because at that time any such statement of contact with the supernatural was liable in Scotland to be interpreted as an admission of witchcraft. Kirk must have known that, and that the penalty for such an offence was capital punishment through the cruellest form of death by being 'worried', that is strangled at the stake, before being burnt to death. Despite this he appears to have had such conviction about what he believed he had seen that he recorded it all in minute detail in *The Secret Commonwealth*.

Printed versions of Kirk's book have been published twice, once in Victorian times and again in the 1930s. As well as reading what Kirk wrote, it is also possible to follow his mysterious nightly route from the old manse through the woods to Doon Hill, where the rough path to the summit is now whimsically marked with signs bearing little fairy mushrooms. At the top of Fairy Hill, as it is often known, the exact spot where the minister was spirited away by the fairies is said to be marked by the tallest tree, a solitary Scots pine which soars skyward amongst the surrounding oaks.

Over the years there have been many attempts to explain the strange disappearance of Mr Kirk, many of them focusing upon the fact that Aberfoyle is situated right on the Highland Boundary Fault, the massive geological crack which runs diagonally across Scotland from Arbroath on the east coast to Toward Point at the foot of the Cowal Peninsula in Argyll and on across the estuary of the river Clyde to Rothesay on the Isle of Bute in the west. At Aberfoyle the fault line very clearly and visibly separates the rugged Highlands to the north-west from the Lowlands to the south-east and it is suggested that such a crack may also be a route into the underworld with which the Revd Kirk came into such close contact.

Those interested in the supernatural who come to inspect Mr Kirk's long, red sandstone tombstone in the graveyard near the banks of the Forth at Aberfoyle, are also fascinated by the heavy cast-iron, coffin-shaped mort safes which lie by the entrance to the ruins of the old church. Despite their French-sounding name, it was in Scottish kirkyards that mort safes became a necessity, about a century after the Aberfoyle minister's strange demise, because of the threat posed by the resurrectionists, body snatchers like the infamous Burke and Hare, who made a good living stealing newly buried corpses from the grave and delivering them to the professors of anatomy at Edinburgh, Glasgow and St Andrews Universities to allow their medical students to practise dissecting them and thus enabling them to learn about the workings of the human body. These heavy iron devices were placed over the graves after a burial to make it more difficult for the body snatchers, or corpse vandals as they were also called, to do their sordid work. The mort safes were kept in position for three weeks, by which time the body of the deceased was no longer saleable to the anatomists, the freshest corpses fetching the highest prices!

It is this latter point which creates great interest amongst believers in the supernatural who visit the graveyard at Aberfoyle. Why, they ask, would body snatchers choose to rob graves in such a remote churchyard, when there are many situated much closer to the city of Glasgow from which they would have had a much better chance of delivering the corpses fresh to the slab in the anatomy theatre of the university the following morning, thus gaining for them the best price on offer? Why, they go on to demand, are there no similar mort safes in other graveyards in the Trossachs apart from the examples to be seen at Aberfoyle? This leads them on to claim that the Aberfoyle mort safes were not purchased by the village kirk's board to thwart body snatchers, who never came, but were bought at considerable expense because, even a century after the minister's disappearance, the parishioners were still scared that the district's wee folk would return some night to spirit away another of their number.

In *The Secret Commonwealth*, Mr Kirk does indeed make several mentions of other people on Doon Hill being spirited away by the fairies, but, unlike him, they all always later re-emerged in a dazed state on another part of its slopes, unable to remember anything of what they had seen in the underworld of the wee folk. All of these reports lead modern students of the supernatural to suggest that Aberfoyle may be particularly liable to time travel, because it lies in an area where electromagnetic forces are especially strong as a result of the geological fault line. Could this, they ponder, be why Mr Kirk was so insistent that if Graham of Duchray threw a knife, he would be able to step back into the present from the fairy time trap in which he was ensnared? Could the Aberfoyle minister have been centuries ahead of his time in understanding about the earth's magnetic field and have intended the metal knife to create a short circuit?

Yet others suggest that Mr Kirk's involvement with the fairies, fauns, elves and brownies came about not from such modern thoughts but from his involvement with the most ancient craft of the Masons. Kirk was known to be a member and those who follow this line of thought are sure that much of what he wrote in *The Secret Commonwealth* was derived from the rites of Freemasonry.

Coming much more firmly down to earth, before leaving the cemetery at Kirkton of Aberfoyle it is worth taking time to browse amongst the other grave-stones to read the inscriptions on them and thus discover about the lives and occupations of those villagers who lie buried there. Note how many children died in infancy because of the prevalence of infectious diseases.

When Aberfoyle was situated around the old kirk, its name was originally spelt Eperpuil, meaning the village at the mouth of the boggy water, which is an excellent description of this site at the mouth of the Phu Burn, or Poo Burn as it is pronounced and as it appears to be printed on modern maps. The earliest recorded mention of Eperpuil occurred as long ago as the sixth century, when

St Berach of Tormonberry visited Aedan, King of the Scots, and was granted Aedan's fort as his headquarters in Alba. It is intriguing to wonder whether, as Eperpuil was mentioned at this time, the stronghold could possibly have been the one on Doon Hill. In later records, Eperpuil becomes Eperphuille, then Eperfuil, Eperfoil and Eperfoyle until the coming of the railway in the 1880s, with its published maps, timetables and guides, standardised the spelling as Aberfoyle, just as the spread of the trains did to place names in many other parts of Scotland.

In Aberfoyle, however, the building of the track for the steam trains had an even more dramatic effect than changing the spelling of the name, as the siting of the new station resulted in the effective resiting of the centre of the village.

Thus Aberfoyle's transition from its origins around the kirk to where it is situated now, on the opposite bank of the river Forth at the foot of the Limecraig and Craigmore hills, can be credited to the coming of the railway. The new line was brought to the village in 1884 not primarily as a means of transporting visitors, as was the case with the line through Callander, but to carry slates from the quarry up on the Duke's Pass; slates were in great demand for the roofing of the many tenements – the tight-packed Victorian answer to modern blocks of high-rise flats – which were needed to house Glasgow's expanding nineteenth-century population.

It was only the great value of this profitable year-round goods traffic which prompted the construction of the railway line from Bucklyvie north to Aberfoyle, because it was a very difficult task to achieve as a result of the marshy, peaty bog land which it had to cross. Previous to this, Victorian visitors travelling by train who wished to enter the Trossachs via Aberfoyle, rather than making a roundtrip from Callander, travelled north by rail from Glasgow and alighted at the halt at Arnprior. From there they completed their journey to Aberfoyle by road in one of the horse-drawn omnibuses which awaited their arrival in the station forecourt. The enterprising station master at Arnprior even cashed in on this business by producing one of the earliest guidebooks to the area. Interestingly as long ago as the 1870s he clearly recognised that a good story could help sell his book and increase interest in the area, because he was at pains to emphasise Aberfoyle as a very mystical, magical district and the capital of the kingdom of Scotland's fairy folk. At last, however, the new line was completed all the way to Aberfoyle in 1884, but many local people still had grave doubts about its safety because of the treacherous, wet, boggy land across which the new track had been laid. To prove its worthiness, therefore, it was decided that the first train to reach Aberfoyle should have its wagons filled with ballast made up of red sandstone, the reasoning being that if the track survived such a test with such a weighty load, it could definitely cope with the heaviest loads of slate which the trains running over it were intended thereafter to convey.

The new line survived this trial and the wagons full of sandstone arrived safely at Aberfoyle Railway Station, which stood on the site of the large car park between Main Street and the river Forth. The problem then was what to do with the cargo of stones. Instead of going to the expense of transporting them out again, or incurring a loss of revenue by simply leaving them in a large pile beside the track, it was decided to sell them off cheaply; thus many buildings around Aberfoyle are constructed of red sandstone, including the block which now houses the premises of the Bank of Scotland and Craiguchty, the eye-catching Tudor-style terrace in Main Street. Its equally unusual name comes from that which this part of the district bore before it became known as Aberfoyle, a result of that name being chosen for the new station and appearing in the railway timetables.

Not everyone in Aberfoyle welcomed the coming of the railway. Some of the local farmers complained that its long embankment caused their fields to flood. They were so enraged that they started to try to dig a hole through the new embankment, but were thwarted in their efforts when they came up against rock. They then threatened to blow a hole in it using explosives, but fortunately for the new railway were again prevented from doing so, this time by their inability to afford to purchase sufficient dynamite!

Over a hundred years later the now long-disused railway embankment still causes flooding problems and in March 1999 the Roads Department of Stirling Council, which is now the local government authority responsible for the whole of the Trossachs, constructed a culvert through the old railway embankment, where the burn comes tumbling down the hillside next to the new medical centre, in yet another bid to reduce the problem of water blocking the main road.

Apart from the old embankment, other traces of the railway still remain, including the low line of cottages built by the railway company to accommodate the station master, booking clerk, porters and their families. The station master occupied the slightly larger house at the end of the row, which overlooks the children's playground and playing field and which can be seen from Main Street opposite the garage. As a single-track line, the railway to Aberfoyle required a turntable to turn the locomotive and its wagons or passenger carriages, ready for the return journey south to Glasgow, and in the wooded area just beyond the car park the marks of where it operated can still be found. The route of the line itself is also still well preserved, as the track bed has been converted into a well-maintained footpath stretching east parallel to the main road, which provides a pleasant walk to the Rob Roy Motel.

The coming of the railway to Aberfoyle in the 1880s did not do away with the village's carriage trade, because the old wooden wagonettes and horse-drawn buses were still needed to convey the ever-increasing numbers of Victorian visitors, who wanted to explore the Trossachs. Old pictures of the entrance to the railway station show these well-packed vehicles with their teams of horses about to depart for various local beauty spots. Many of them were based right at the foot of the Duke's Pass at the famous Bailie Nicol Jarvie Inn. Once the most famous hotel in the whole area it was named after the legendary Glasgow magistrate who wielded a red hot poker, drawn straight from the fire, as the handiest weapon available to scatter his attackers. The scene was made famous by Sir Walter Scott in his book *Rob Roy* and is still vividly and colourfully depicted in the painting above the front entrance to the old building.

POPULAR DRIVES & WALKS

TO

Scenes of "The Lady of the Lake" & Romance of "Rob Roy."

1. Old Clachan of Aberfoyle—½ mile.
2. Historic Pass of Aberfoyle, leading up to Loch Ard—1½ miles.
3. The Bailie's Rock and Tree, and famous Cave of Rob Roy—3 miles.
4. Ledard Fall—4½ miles.
5. Lochs Dhu and Chon, "in the birch-grown beauty of the hills"—7 miles.
6. Lake Menteith, with its island ruins of Inchmahome, famous in Scottish history as the refuge of Queen Mary.
7. Lovely Circular Drive by Duchray's Old Castle and Glasgow Corporation Water Works' Aqueduct, and round Loch Ard, commanding magnificent view of the Loch on the route—13¾ miles.
8. Circular Drive by Lake Menteith, Cardross, Arnprior, Buchlyvie, Gartartan Peel, Flanders Moss, and Gartmore—20 miles.
9. Circular Drive to Trossachs, Callander, and Lake Menteith—27 miles.
10. Circular Walk by Camahlatair Waterfall, and back by Craigmore, with fine view of the Aberfoyle Valley.
11. Lovely Walk to Milton and Duchry Castle—6 miles.
12. Circular Walk by Fairy Knowe and Gartmore Bridge—4 miles.
13. Crags of Ben Venue, Craig More, Craig Vat, and Meull Ear—all in walking distance.
14. Beautiful Drives to—
    Stronachlachar, ... 12 miles.
    Callander, ... 12 „
    Inversnaid Falls on Loch Lomond side, 16 „
    Stirling Castle, ... 20 „

Tours from the Bailie Nicol Jarvie were extensive, even in 1890. Horse-drawn carriages full of day trippers were often seen pulling away from the hotel until the early 1920s. (J. & C. McCutcheon)

Above Aberfoyle's well-known Bailie Nicol Jarvie Hotel has now been converted into private houses. The painting of the famous 'Affray At Aberfoyle', as described by Sir Walter Scott in his novel *Rob Roy*, has been preserved and can be seen above the main entrance. (William F. Hendrie)

Right The Bailie Nicol Jarvie Hotel, *c*.1890, having just been rebuilt. (J. & C. McCutcheon)

The Hotel has just been completely rebuilt and refurnished in modern style.

VIEW OF HOTEL.

Historic though the former hotel building is, it only dates from Victorian times, however, and the fight commemorated in oils really took place some distance away at an earlier drovers' inn. There the Highlanders who accompanied the cattle from the north used to pause to enjoy a wee refreshment, while their equally thirsty beasts enjoyed a drink in the Forth, before fording the river and being driven south to the markets or trysts at Larbert and Falkirk.

Like the previous drovers' inn, sadly the 'Bailie Nic', as it was familiarly known to its local patrons in Aberfoyle, has also ceased to operate as a hotel and it has now been converted into spacious private apartments. From the outside, however, the old building still looks much the same, occupying the most prominent corner site in the village at the foot of the hill and, with the exception of the red painted poker which for countless years hung from a ring embedded in the trunk of an ancient oak tree in the hotel garden and was always pointed out as the one which the courageous Bailie had wielded, it is still possible to see many features of the exterior, linking it with the days when it was at the height of its popularity in coaching times. Then there were often as many as sixty horses in its stables, ready to haul the coaches taking guests on their steep climbs into the hills.

Some of the older men in Aberfoyle, including local historian Ian Nicholson, still remember how as boys they used to earn pennies to add to their holiday pocket money by stationing themselves strategically at the steepest points on the Duke's Pass, ready to nip out and shove heavy wooden blocks, called chocks, below the wagonette wheels to stop them rolling backwards when the horses had to pause for a much-needed rest as they tackled the long, twisting ascent.

The days of the horse-drawn coaches and buses did not come to an end until the mid-1930s, when a work creation programme to help local unemployed men find work greatly improved the gradient and surface of the road, which allowed more of the increasing number of cars and motorbuses on Scottish roads to negotiate its tight bends. At the same time the Duke's Pass, built originally by the Duke of Montrose to reach his hunting lodge at Loch Achray, ceased to be a toll road, but the toll house where the money was formerly collected at the Aberfoyle end can still be seen at the start of the steep hill leading out of the village. It stands on the left as the hill starts to rise and is still called The Toll House.

Horses, or rather sturdy Highland ponies, reappeared in Aberfoyle shortly after the Second World War in the late 1940s and 1950s when the village vied with Newtonmore in Speyside for the title of birthplace of the new sport of pony trekking. In Aberfoyle this exciting new sport was developed by the well-known Hugh MacGregor of Balanton, and soon long lines of ponies patiently bearing their novice riders became a popular sight as they plodded their way along Main Street every morning and evening at the start and finish of their day-long treks into the surrounding hills and forests. Some of the ponies were housed at Kirkton Stables, others at the stables on the hillside above the Bailie Nicol Jarvie, while others were quartered at the Covenanters Inn, Aberfoyle's other famous landmark hotel, which was always a popular base for the trekkers.

With its long row of whitewashed buildings straddling the wooded hillside overlooking the river Forth, the Covenanters, which was originally the private holiday home of a well-to-do Glasgow family, became known in the 1960s as The Ponderosa, after the popular American cowboy television series of the era. Nowadays most of its horses have gone, but unlike the Bailie Nicol Jarvie, the Covenanters Inn, with its tartan-carpeted restaurant and lounges and open log fires, oak beams and snug inglenook bars, is still a busy tourist hotel and its weekend dinner dances in the ballroom are a popular feature of local life.

The hotel takes its unusual name not from the Scottish Protestant religious stalwarts who in the seventeenth century defied the king's efforts to make them worship in the fashion of the Episcopalian Church in England and, rather than submit, left their churches and took to worshipping at secret open-air conventicles in the hills, including those around Aberfoyle, as is described in chapter eight, but from a much more modern group of Scots who called themselves the Covenanters and met in the late 1940s. They planned for the day when Scotland would once more be an independent country and in 1949 signed a covenant to achieve this. These Nationalists included the then owner of the hotel and, shortly afterwards, the Covenanters became involved in one of the most romantic incidents in modern Scottish history, for when the Stone of Destiny disappeared from below the coronation throne in Westminster Abbey in the early 1950s, rumour has it that the inn was one of the hideaways where it found a temporary safe resting place.

Another Aberfoyle hotel with a history, although its buildings are more modern, dating from the 1950s, is the Rob Roy at the junction of the A81 road from Glasgow with the B829 through the village, as it claims to have been Scotland's first motel when this American idea crossed the Atlantic. Its separate chalet-style accommodation gained it immediate publicity, for, shortly after it first opened, the seclusion of one of its chalets was chosen by a gang of Glasgow bank robbers as an ideal hiding place to share out the cash which they had stolen.

A few years later the modern structure of the Pavilion in Main Street was added to the list of Aberfoyle hostelries. It still plies its trade, but its pub restaurant is now known by the more appropriate name of the Forth Inn, as it stands right on the shores of the river only a short distance downstream from the first Forth Bridge, as the little old stone humpbacked bridge at Aberfoyle is proudly known.

Opposite the Forth Inn, the Coach House, converted as the name suggests from a former stable block, is another comparatively new addition to Aberfoyle's long list of eating and drinking places. It also offers several well-furnished, comfortable en suite bedrooms. The old Clachan Inn in the heart of the village

The modern lines of the Pavilion, which is now known as the Forth Inn, in the centre of Aberfoyle. (William F. Hendrie)

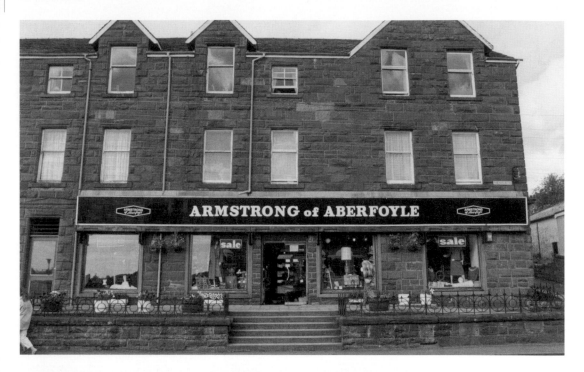

Above Until the 1980s Armstrong of Aberfoyle was the largest and best known store in the village. The building which it occupied was one of those built with the red sandstone brought to the village on a trial run by the first steam train to reach Aberfoyle. (William F. Hendrie).

Left Newspaper delivery boys set off on their rounds past Craigcuthy Terrace in Main Street, Aberfoyle, another of the local buildings constructed of the red sandstone transported by the first train to reach the village as a test of the strength of the new railway track across the moss lands to the south of the village. (William F. Hendrie)

in Main Street, has recently been modernised but still provides a friendly, homely atmosphere in which to enjoy a meal in its upstairs restaurant or a drink in its downstairs bar. On the outskirts of Aberfoyle, several of the Victorian villas which line the Loch Ard Road have also been converted into attractive small hotels, such as the Inverard and the Altskeith. There are in addition many well-run bed and breakfast establishments in and around the village. The latest information about them can be obtained from the Trossachs Centre at the entrance to the car park in Main Street, which, in addition to its excellent displays about the area and its children's indoor playground featuring a model of the Trossachs Trundler veteran bus, also houses an information bureau, with

Above McCallum's Clachan Hotel in Main Street, Aberfoyle, originally shared its ground floor with the village's licensed grocers' shop. Here postcards, such as this one from 1920, could be purchased and sent the world over. (J. & C. McCutcheon)

Right Aberfoyle still has its village butcher. Next door the former fish and chip shop was once known as The Red Herring. (William F. Hendrie)

a staff who are very knowledgeable about which of the houses in the village have rooms to let and which are most suitable for different visitors, from couples to family groups.

Many more visitors to Aberfoyle, however, stay not in its many hotels and bed and breakfasts, but at the village's well-known Dounans Residential Outdoor Education Centre, situated high above the village on the edge of the Queen Elizabeth Forest Park. Originally known simply as 'the camp', Dounans dates back to 1940 and the start of the Second World War. During the months leading up to the outbreak of the war in September 1939, the government was worried that a repetition of the blitz air-raid tactics used by the Germans during the

Aberfoyle Main Street. (William F. Hendrie)

recent Spanish Civil War would endanger the lives of children living in British cities, which would be likely targets for enemy attack. Not wanting to panic the civilian population, it was proposed by the Camps Act of 25 May 1939 to build residential schools in rural settings throughout England and Scotland, allegedly to further the 1930s cult for outdoor education, but in reality to be ready to evacuate thousands of children.

Thirty-two sites were chosen in England from Sussex north to Lancashire and five in Scotland, two to serve Glasgow, two to cater for children from Edinburgh and one to cope with children from Dundee. Of the two sites for the camps to be hurriedly built in the west of Scotland, it was decided that one should be on the lands of Upper Dounans Croft, tucked away in the hills behind Aberfoyle. Such was the haste to build the camps that the Act gave powers of compulsory purchase and stated that planning permission was not needed for the erection of the required accommodation. To expedite construction still further, it was decided that all thirty-seven school camps should be built to the same design, detail varying only in the siting of the dormitories, assembly hall and other buildings.

With the actual outbreak of hostilities on Sunday 3 September 1939, the work of erecting the camps was given a new urgency. In England it was entrusted to the National Camp Corporation acting for the Ministry of Health and in Scotland it was the first task given to the newly formed Scottish Special Housing Association (SSHA).

Again it is interesting to note that the SSHA received its instructions from the Department of Health for Scotland and that initially the Education Department at the Scottish Office had no connection with the five camps built north of the border at Broomlee near West Linton in Peebleshire, Middleton Hall near Gorebridge in Midlothian, Glengonnar near Abington in the Southern Uplands of Lanarkshire, Belmont Estate near Meigle and at Dounans, Aberfoyle, the two last of which were at that time in Perthshire.

The first of the Scottish Camps to be completed was Broomlee, and Dounans followed shortly afterwards in the autumn of 1940. Like the others, it had accommodation for 360 children in six long redwood dormitory blocks, which like all of the other buildings in the camp were roofed with wooden shingles. Each dormitory slept sixty boys or sixty girls in rows of double metal bunks in two areas separated by a central wooden partition, with thirty-two boys or girls on one side and twenty-eight on the other. At each end there were two narrow single rooms for teachers, with small windows looking into the dormitories so that they could keep a watchful eye on their charges, whose every move they could also hear as there was no sound-proofing in the thin walls. In the centre of each dormitory block, a wooden lean-to shed-like addition housed two toilets. One was reserved for use by the four teachers who lived in the block and both were strictly reserved for use during the night. There were large double doors at the entrance to each end of the dormitories and, no matter what the weather, these were hooked open each morning to ventilate the whole block. In the central partition between the two dormitories there was a small communicating door, and it says much for the standard of discipline amongst Scottish children in the 1940s that this provision was intended by the planners to allow one teacher to supervise all sixty youngsters after lights out!

Once the children were bedded down for the night and the blackout blinds pulled tight closed, a single blue-painted electric bulb was left switched on in the centre of each dormitory and its eerie glow no doubt gave rise to the persistent tale that Dounans Residential Outdoor Educaton Centre is home to a resident ghost. She is known as the Blue Lady and she does indeed seem to be a 'Lady of the Lamp', as she is often reported as being glimpsed making her way across from the little chalet-like sickbay to one or other of the long dormitory blocks as though intent, like the camp nurse, on ensuring that all of the children are safe and well and sleeping in their bunks. Certainly in all of the sixty years that sightings have been reported, none has ever alleged that she intends any harm to the many youngsters who have enjoyed staying there.

The first children to come to the camp at Aberfoyle were wee evacuees from Glasgow. The 'vaccies', as they were soon nicknamed, arrived within days of the completion of construction of the camp and soon Dounans was full to capacity, although numbers had later to be reduced to 300 following a disastrous blaze. Fortunately the fire caused no injuries amongst the pupils, but it did totally destroy one of the six dormitory blocks as a result of lack of water to fight the flames, despite the fact that it was situated on the west side of the camp on the banks of the burn, the little rocky stream which has proved a popular feature of life at Dounans for generations of Scottish bairns. The classroom attached to the dormitory block was saved and still stands on the west side of the camp.

Although originally intended only to last for a maximum of ten years, the five remaining dormitory blocks still survive. From the outside, apart from the addition of covered verandas, they look much the same as they did when they were first constructed sixty years ago. In contrast, inside they have been modernised and their interior space converted into four twelve-bed chalets each with three cubicles, a teacher's room and en suite facilities for both pupils and staff. Carpeted and curtained, they have brought a touch of comfort to camping.

'We're off to the camp in country, hurrah, hurrah' runs the wartime song, but in reality life at Dounans for the evacuees was far from fun and frolics in the countryside. The school camp was run on strict boarding school lines, with réveillé each morning at 7.30 a.m. For its period the camp was considered very modern with coke-fired central heating and two central ablutions blocks with toilets, handbasins and what was described at the time as 'communal sprays'. Children were strictly forbidden from entering the sprays, or showers, on their own and were paraded to them in groups three times a week either before breakfast or before bedtime. The sight of these pyjama and nightgown-clad children all clutching towels and washbags became a familiar one at Dounans.

At mealtimes all of the children were assembled in front of the dining hall, where hands were inspected before they marched in to their places at long tables with benches for eight on either side. No food was served until all 360 boys and girls were seated in silence with heads bowed for grace to be said. One child from each table then trooped up to the servery and carried two plates of food back to place in front of the others. With wartime rationing in force, there was no question of any choice of menu and no thought of separate dishes for vegetarians, who were in any case practically unknown amongst the Glasgow bairns. Although food was basic the children always had enough to eat, with plenty of good creamy milk delivered from local dairies. Apart from a cooked breakfast, lunch and an evening meal, the day was always rounded off with supper consisting of mugs of steaming hot cocoa, prepared in enormous tall jugs on top of the stoves in the kitchen and served with jammy pieces. The flavour of the bright red jam was always a mystery, many of the evacuees insisting it definitely was not strawberry, raspberry or even bramble, but more probably turnip! These jammy or jelly pieces, as the bairns – children – often called them, however were sweet and satisfying, and ensured that they never went to bed with an empty stomach when the bell for lights out was rung at what to modern children would seem the unbelievably early hour of 8.30 p.m.

While the children all ate together at their long tables in the big dining room, the teachers, apart from those on meals duty, were served in a partitioned-off section at the end of the dining room with an open fireplace, where they sat at tables covered with white cloths and were waited upon by black-uniformed maids, who later poured tea in the adjoining staffroom. Like the camp domestic staffroom at the other end of the dining hall, it also had an open coal-fired grate.

Immediately after breakfast medical parade took place at the camp's own little sickbay, with its own dispensary and small wards. It was staffed by a qualified nurse, supported by the local Aberfoyle GP. The doctor was paid a small retainer for his services and was always attentive to the needs of his many young patients.

Each school day then began at 9.00 a.m. with worship and prayers in the assembly hall across the open veranda from which was situated the headmaster's office, outside whose door any miscreants were ordered to line up and wait at the end of the service. While discipline was of the old fashioned kind, the classrooms where the children were taught were considered very modern, with a public address system through which the headmaster could address all of the pupils and staff and through which the new-fangled BBC Schools radio programmes, such as 'Singing Together' and 'Music and Movement', could be broadcast. The classrooms were lined on either side by large windows, very different from the tall narrow ones of the traditional Glasgow schools, and in a publication printed two years after the end of the war in 1947, the rooms were described as 'sun traps'.

Dounans was also well provided with sports and leisure facilities, including a large football field, a rounders pitch, a tarmac tennis and netball court and a play park with see-saws, roundabout and several sets of swings. Most importantly perhaps for the children, the camp had its own tuck shop, where they were allowed to use up their ration coupons to buy the few available bars of chocolate, sweets and lollipops. Apart from the little shop beside the assembly hall, the children were also allowed once a week to walk in crocodile to the shops in the village, while on Sunday mornings they paraded to Aberfoyle parish church.

While the authorities prayed that the children would be safe from bombing in their rural hideaway, no chances were taken and concrete-roofed brick air-raid shelters were built on several sites in the camp, where the remains of some of them can still be seen. At last, however, in May 1945 peace was declared and the evacuees were able to go back to their homes. As the fleet of buses sent to collect them disappeared in a swirl of dust down the forest track, the elated youngsters may well have sung what became the camp's unofficial anthem during those long years of hostilities, 'Build a bonfire, build a bonfire, put the heidie on the top, put the teachers round about him and we'll burn the blooming lot!'

Dounans did not, however, lie idle for long, as it was soon pressed into service again to house child refugees from the Netherlands. These boys and girls from Holland apparently never forgot the warm welcome which they received at Dounans, because in 1996 a large group of them returned, exactly fifty years later, for a reunion and to see again the place in Scotland which had offered them freedom and happiness after the grim years of wartime occupation in their own land. Before they left they presented a plaque, which records their thanks for their post-war stay in Aberfoyle, and it is displayed outside the assembly hall at Dounans.

By 1947 reconstruction in Holland had progressed sufficiently for the children to return to their homes and, for the first time, Dounans school camp was able to provide the service for which it had been officially designed in the 1930s. At about this same time, the thirty-two similar camps in England were handed over to the local authorities in whose territories they happened to have been built. Although some of these education authorities took interest in them and made more use of them than others, few have survived. Fortunately in Scotland a different policy was followed and the Education Department created

the Scottish National Camps Association to administer all five sites and make them available to the nation's children irrespective of where they came from.

Dounans was used in particular by West Lothian, Midlothian, Edinburgh, Clackmannanshire, Renfrewshire, Fife, Lanarkshire and Dundee, each authority devising its own pattern of attendance. West Lothian favoured week-long stays in July to provide pupils with holidays which their families could not otherwise have afforded, while Clackmannanshire chose month-long periods in term time and ran the camp much more like a boarding school. Edinburgh created its own permanent school camp staff, complete with headmaster, and took primary pupils to camp for two weeks in term time. Dundee used its residential stays at Dounans for music camps at which many enthusiastic young players experienced the pleasure of playing together as an orchestra, before giving a concert on the final evening.

The cost of coming to stay at Dounans in the 1950s was as low as 10s (50p) for a whole week and, where parents could not afford that amount, it was paid for by the local authorities. In many cases teachers gave their services without pay so that their pupils could benefit from these weeks away from home amongst the hills of the Trossachs. Amongst those who volunteered to give up several weeks of summer holidays to serve at Dounans was Bo'ness Academy history teacher Tam Dalyell, who soon afterwards became Member of Parliament for West Lothian, an area he still serves almost forty years later as representative for the Linlithgow constituency. In between teaching and becoming a politician, Tam wrote 'The Case for Ship Schools', an idea taken up by the British India Steam Navigation Co. Ltd, on whose first school ship, MS *Dunera*, he became Depute Director of Education and was able to put into practice on the high seas ideas he had first learned during his spells of residential education at Aberfoyle.

Dounans Outdoor Education Centre seen in this view taken in 1967, looking west to Craigmore, was originally opened in 1940 to accommodate wartime evacuee children from Glasgow. (Photograph by Scott Guthrie Pollock, who was for many years Headmaster of the West Lothian Summer Holiday Camps held at Aberfoyle)

While it is sad that the British government so disgracefully allowed the school ship project to be sunk by the Falklands War, it is good that Dounans survived other threats in the 1980s and has now grown into a fully fledged modern outdoor education centre. Run by Scottish Centres, it offers exciting adventure and environmental study courses not only to primary and secondary pupils, but also to adults. They range from members of the Salvation Army and Mormon churches to those sent by firms to enjoy the challenge of its management training weeks.

Now, in addition to the playing fields and open spaces which it has always possessed, Dounans provides facilities for activities ranging from abseiling to problem solving, orienteering, hill walking and it even has its own canoe pond, designed as an exercise by the soldiers of the Royal Corps of Engineers, where beginners can gain confidence before venturing out onto the surrounding lochs and rivers of the Trossachs. The army also provided Dounans with an open-air amphitheatre and barbecue site, carved out of the hillside, and it was there in May 1995 that a campfire sing-song was held to commemorate the fiftieth anniversary of the coming of Peace in Europe.

Many ingenious costumes were conjured up by the pupils who took part in this fancy dress parade on the lawn in the middle of the main square at Dounans on this warm Wednesday evening in July 1967. (Scott Guthrie Pollock)

Twenty years later in 1987 the dormitory blocks at Dounans were converted into chalets, each with its own veranda-covered entrance. The modernised outdoor centre was officially re-opened by Scottish Minister for Education, Michael Forsyth MP, who had his home locally at Loch Ard and who later went on to become Secretary of State for Scotland and was rewarded with a knighthood. (William F. Hendrie)

Much of the attraction of Dounans, however, lies not in its man-made attractions, but from its natural setting in the hills, which offer so many opportunities for walking, orienteering and all-terrain biking. Directly behind Dounans, on the steep slopes of Limecraig, it is also possible to try the exciting sport of gully scrambling. This is a simplified version of gorge walking, the popular Scottish outdoor adventure activity pioneered by Dr Tom Pacey of Ullapool. While gorge walking challenges participants to climb up a waterfall, gully scrambling involves climbing up the bed of a Highland burn and, at the same time as having soaking wet muddy fun, getting to know about its ecology. The credit for developing gully scrambling at Aberfoyle belongs to Alastair Marquis, who, when he was Head of Bankton primary school in Livingston, West Lothian, introduced hundreds of pupils to this outdoor pursuit and who, as Inspector of Schools at the Scottish Office Department of Education, still champions the cause of outdoor education both as part of formal education and as part of the informal sector such as the programme provided by the Boys' Brigade, to which he has devoted much of his leisure time.

With such muddy activities as gully scrambling and tackling its assault course available as attractions, it is fortunate that the modern Dounans is well equipped with hot showers, clothes washing facilities and drying rooms. Other up-to-date indoor facilities include art and craft rooms, while for evening entertainment the assembly hall is equipped with a disco.

Over the years highlights of the many seasons at Dounans have included playing host to the 1969 Scottish International Youth Camp and several YMCA international weeks involving as many as fifteen different nationalities. BP's Grizzly Challenge has also chosen Dounans as the setting for its Scottish rounds. The largest of all the events ever held at Dounans was the first ever International Challenger Competition to be held in Britain, during which over 900 adult competitors and officials were catered for on the site.

Dounans has been honoured with a royal visit when Queen Elizabeth the Queen Mother flew in by helicopter on 24 September 1973, on the occasion of the unveiling of the stone cairn dedicated to her in the grounds of the Forest Centre, where it stands in front of the lodge building. Dounans has also been visited by the Lord High Commissioner to the General Assembly of the Church of Scotland and his Purse Bearer. They were pictured in the next morning's papers looking on as a pupil showed them the bishop from the set of pieces for the camp's large open-air chessboard and a headline read, 'A Bishop for the Kirk?'

While Dounans has served well the many groups who have come to enjoy it for over half a century, so too have the participants in them, in turn, benefited the village economy by buying goods in Aberfoyle's shops and patronising local services, from the fish and chip shop to the curio shop which now occupies the premises of the former licensed grocers, to the many boutiques and the Green Art Gallery. In addition, their attendance at Dounans has made the Outdoor Centre one of the largest employers in the area, providing jobs ranging from outdoor instructors to gardeners and maintenance men to cooks, cleaners and office staff, all jobs important in a rural area such as the Trossachs.

Best known of the managers at Dounans was undoubtedly Bob Ralston, who was in charge for thirty years from 1965 to 1995 and oversaw all of the work of upgrading the camp into what is now without question one of the best outdoor education centres in Britain. There could have been no better choice than Bob, with his Boys' Brigade background, to lead Dounans forward as an outdoor adventure centre. Bob was very much a man of the hills and he was always ready and willing to share his knowledge and love of them with the teachers and pupils who came to the centre. Equally well loved by the many guests at Dounans were his dogs, who were always by his side as he went about his work and his daily round of the camp. Four were golden retrievers: Cruachan, his mate Scoobie and their pups Duke and Isla. Cruachan was a trained search and rescue dog who accompanied Bob when he was called out as a member of the local mountain rescue team. The retrievers were always calm and patient and endured endless hours of petting from the thousands of children who stayed at the camp and became their instant friends. The presence of Cruachan, Scoobie, Duke and Isla did indeed help many of the youngsters overcome any initial feelings of homesickness. Bob's other dog, Tramp, was an adopted mongrel who was altogether a different and much noisier character, but the children soon discovered that while he barked a lot he never bit and they soon became friends with him too. Dounans could not in fact have had a finer watchdog than Trampie, whose bark gave warning of any stranger who chanced up the forest drive from the main road, long before he entered the camp.

Looking back over his long career at Dounans, Bob recalls many highlights, including the week of the Scottish International Youth Camp in July 1969, when he offered to teach a group of young participants fly-casting, and some of the

Canoeing lessons at the Dounans Outdoor Education Centre. (William F. Hendrie)

wettest weather he had ever known turned the lawn of his home into a ready-made improvised loch.

Dounans could, however, also enjoy good spells of dry weather and one particular sunny summer week, which Bob remembers with equally warm affection, was when he was faced with the challenge of integrating six very different groups who had never met before coming to camp. They included two parties of Egyptian school pupils from Cairo and Alexandria, a party of boys and girls from Paris, whose parents were employees of Air France, a group of German Boy Scouts, several classes of English children from Framwellgate Comprehensive School in County Durham and a group of mentally disabled Scottish youngsters from Edinburgh. During that August week Bob introduced all of the youngsters to each other by sharing with them his love for Scottish dancing and it was agreed that on their final evening they would all share in a ceilidh in the assembly hall. While the ceilidh was at its energetic height, Bob was called out to welcome the members of the first of the following week's groups, who he knew had travelled all the way from the south of Ireland. To his surprise they turned out to be members of a pipe band going on the following day to play in the competitions at the Cowal Highland Gathering at Dunoon. Travel weary though they were as they clambered off their bus, they heard the sounds of the ceilidh and instead of going off to their dormitories to get some rest before the big day, they quickly unpacked their pipes and drums from the boot of the bus and marched straight into the hall to provide an unexpectedly rousing, but much appreciated, finale to the evening's proceedings.

'I always considered that Dounans was all about learning to live together and the atmosphere on that summer night amongst those diverse groups truly captured for me, all that life at camp could achieve,' said Bob. 'Conceived as a necessity of the war years, Dounans has developed into a powerful tool for peace and hopefully the many friendships developed there over more than half a century, will help ensure such hostilities never happen again.'

During his thirty years at Dounans, Bob and his wife Anne, who taught for many years at the village school, practised what they believed in and always participated fully in the life of the camp by living on site in the manager's house, which adjoined the headmaster's house overlooking the camp playing field. With Anne and Bob in residence, the little Swiss chalet-style cottage, with its overhanging eaves, its decorative floral baskets, its immaculately kept garden and its sets of red deer antlers on the walls always drew appreciative glances, not just from residents at Dounans, but also from the many hill walkers who used the camp driveway as an access point to the forest.

At their home at Dounans, the Ralstons' three youngsters, Morag, Eleanor and Malcolm, grew up and learnt to think nothing of having hundreds of different children as new playmates each week. In their retirement Bob and Anne still stay in Aberfoyle and continue to play their part in the life of the village and its church.

One of the most attractive features of the modern Dounans Residential Outdoor Education Centre is the pleasant little picnic area which has been created on the hillside adjacent to the canoe pond, and the area's huge boulders are a reminder that as well as its contribution to the history of the twentieth century, this site also has connections with the more distant past. The boulders, for instance, are a reminder that they were dropped here by the slowly melting, retreating glacier, which was no longer able to carry them at the end of the last great Scottish Ice Age.

Nearby, where the sets of children's swings were situated on the hilltop, is thought to have been the site of Dounans Castle. Owned by the Graham family, who also held the stronghold of Duchray Castle 3 miles to the west of Aberfoyle, it is thought to have been a simple tall, square, thick stone-walled peel tower, with its entrance on the first floor for protection and castellated battlements round the roof for further defence.

The castle at Dounans was destroyed by government troops from Stirling Castle after a local seventeenth-century skirmish known as the Battle of The Pass. This running battle took place over two days in October 1653, when the redcoat dragoons, under their commander Colonel Reid, caught up with a party of MacGregor clansmen on the shores of Loch Ard. On the first day the MacGregors, with the backing of Graham of Duchray, managed to hold off the government soldiers. On the second day however the government troops were supplemented by horsemen and the MacGregors and their Graham supporters were forced to retreat. According to local tradition, on their journey back to their barracks at Stirling the dragoons set fire to and destroyed Dounans Castle, so that it could never again be used as a stronghold by their enemies in Strathard. Although details of this engagement between the outlawed MacGregors and the government forces of law and order are scant, the villa near Loch Ard which is called The Pass is a reminder of the battle once fought there.

On the slopes behind the camp it is also possible to find out about more peaceful aspects of Scottish history by examining the remains of Dounans Croft and the early farming methods which were practised there. Before farms became individually owned, they were worked communally through a runrig system, under which local people were allocated by ballot the long narrow strips of parallel land into which both the infield and the more distant outfield were divided. The infield was cultivated intensively, while the outfield was utilised for grazing animals.

Another connection with the history of the area is the site of the lime works from which Limecraig, the wooded hill behind Dounans, takes its name. The lime quarries on the northern side of the hill date back to 1724, when the first written mention of them records that they were being worked by Alexander Graham of Duchray. The demand for lime grew rapidly during the eighteenth century thanks to the Agrarian and Industrial Revolutions. The more modern agricultural methods meant that farmers needed more lime to counter the bleaching effect of rain on their fields, while in industry lime was required by the new processes to manufacture iron. The Aberfoyle lime works continued in operation for well over a century and in 1843 the tenants were McFarlane and

Smoke wafts skywards from cottages on the lower slopes of Limecraig. (William F. Hendrie)

Sorley. By this time, however, the best of the lime had been removed and they were closed down in 1847. The remains of the lime kilns can be traced on the hill above the gate through the boundary fence of the camp.

Another industry which operated on the edge of the camp at Dounans until much more recently was a small timberyard and sawmill situated to the east of the entrance. Today, however, the view from Limecraig is one of undisturbed country calm as it looks out over the fairways and greens of Aberfoyle Golf Course. It is a well-maintained, eighteen-hole course, although some visiting players consider that some of its slopes combine mountaineering with golf. The club is now into its second century and the sepia and black and white photographs on the walls of the clubhouse show groups of enthusiastic early players, the gentlemen in their plus-fours and the ladies in their fashionable billowing Victorian dresses, all carrying their hickory-shafted clubs. Alongside the modern hilltop clubhouse, with its up-to-date facilities including a comfortable bar and dining room with panoramic views of the course, the original Victorian wooden golf pavilion still survives atop the little knowe at the entrance.

On the opposite side of the road in the cluster of old whitewashed farm buildings is the Braeval coffee shop. Long before these modern facilities were established to cater for visitors to Aberfoyle, back in the days when the golf pavilion was built at the 'Entrance to the Trossachs', as the colourful signposts on the approach roads proclaim it to be, the village enjoyed a royal visit from Her Majesty Queen Victoria, and her progress is described in the next chapter.

chapter eight

The Royal Route to Inversnaid

We went on and passed the clachan of Aberfoyle and here the splendid scenery
begins. It is certainly one of the most lovely drives I can remember along Loch Ard,
a fine long loch with trees of all kinds overhanging the road, heather making all
pink, bracken, rocks, high hills of such fine shape and trees growing up them as in
Switzerland. Altogether the whole view was lovely.

Thus wrote Queen Victoria in her journal dated 2 September 1869, and the
journey from Aberfoyle to Inversnaid and Stronachlachar is still as impressively
inspiring today.

As it leaves the village the road passes the present whinstone-built Aberfoyle
parish church, which was first opened the year after the queen's visit in 1870 to
replace the old one on the other side of the river Forth at Kirkton. On its new
site the kirk still overlooks the Forth, which is very much an infant river at this
point on its long journey through the Midland Valley to the North Sea, because
it is not far from this point that it is born through the mingling of the waters of
the Duchray and Avondhu streams. For almost a hundred years the minister
continued to live in the original manse, but now occupies the converted church
hall which is much more conveniently sited just across the road from the
present kirk.

One of the minister's many duties is to act as chaplain to the village school,
which is also situated on this stretch of road, overlooking the river. Very typically
Scottish, it is built of whinstone from the local quarry and its tarmac playground
is surrounded by an iron railing. On the opposite side of the road its playing
field stretches right down to the shore of the river and on a dry warm summer
day as the pupils play on the grass it seems impossible to believe that the Forth
could ever rise to flow right across it and the adjoining road to submerge the
playground on the far side. The land occupied by the playing field is, however,
part of the flood plain of the river and so when the snows melt high on the
shoulders of Ben Lomond and the other surrounding hills, the melt water rapidly

Craigmore rises impressively over Aberfoyle, as seen in this view taken looking west from the school camp at Dounans in 1966. (Scott Guthrie Pollock)

increases the height of the Forth and it does indeed burst its banks and spread across the surrounding flat countryside and into Aberfoyle Main Street. In the past pupils from the primary school sometimes enjoyed the thrill of having to be rowed home from school.

Such excitements were, however, supposed to be part of the history of the village, as Aberfoyle's flood problems were allegedly done away with by an elaborate drainage scheme implemented along the banks of the river during the 1980s. One of the pump houses can be seen by the roadside. In 1998, however, the Forth showed its superior strength. A night when it was already in spate coincided with a strong headwind and high tide further downstream. As a result of this combination of circumstances, the water, prevented from reaching the estuary, backed up and the people of Aberfoyle woke to find Loch Ard Road totally impassable as a result of a flood. The primary school was closed for the day and happily the older brothers and sisters also enjoyed an unexpected holiday as transport was disrupted by other submerged stretches of road all around the village and the school bus could not reach the McLaren High in Callander.

On the hillside beside the school stands the former self-catering Craigmore Outdoor Education Centre. It took its name from the steep hill which rises precipitously above it. 'Craig' means rock and 'more' means big and that well describes it, as its summit does indeed tower 1,271ft above the village. Looking up from Loch Ard Road, its scree-covered slopes make a dramatic sight.

Looking in the other direction can be seen the Duchray Hills, whose slopes are covered with thousands of trees of the Great Forest of Loch Ard, and to the

Skipping and other playground games are still popular with the young pupils at Aberfoyle primary school. The school's solidly constructed whinstone buildings are seen in the background across the tarmac playground. (Arthur Down)

south-west the hump on the horizon is Gualam, which translated from the Gaelic means The Shoulder. This is also an excellent vantage point to look ahead to the west and admire the twin peaks of Ben Lomond. With its impressive height of 3,192ft above sea level, the ben qualifies as one of Scotland's mountains which is classified as a Munro. It is in fact the most southerly of the Munros.

The Great Forest of Loch Ard stretches right up to the lower reaches of the ben and although at first glance it may appear to consist of phalanx upon phalanx of boring conifers, closer inspection reveals a wide variety of both soft and hardwood trees. A good way to explore this extensive forest is to take the clearly way-marked walk, which begins just a little further to the west at Milton. As the name indicates, this is where the waterpower of the Avondhu, which translated from the Gaelic means the Black River, was put to good use in driving the big iron-clad waterwheel. Although no longer in use, it can still be seen outside the old stone-built mill house where the oats used to be ground into meal for such basic staples as porridge and oatcakes.

Milton's links with history go back far further than the solid substantial Victorian villas which line the road, for on the hillside behind their back gardens lies the famous Pulpit Rock. It was here in the seventeenth century that conventicles were held. These were the open-air services held by the Covenanters, who rather than give in to government dictates about praying in the English Episcopalian manner, abandoned their churches and took to worshipping out of doors on the Scottish hillsides. One of the favourite places for such services was here at Milton, where Pulpit Rock provided the ideal site

Solidly built stone villas line Loch Ard Road. Their Victorian scullery and wash houses still jut out on either side, although now converted to more modern uses. (William F. Hendrie)

from which the minister could preach. Access to the rock is from the little cave below and then through a narrow crevice, which climbers would call a chimney. This made Pulpit Rock an ideal preacher's stane, as secrecy was all important at the conventicles. All the time that the minister gave his sermon and conducted the service, lookouts were posted and they were able to give early warning of the approach of the government redcoat soldiers who tried to hunt down the Covenanters. Using secret signals, such as the distinctive cry of the curlew, lookouts could sound the alarm while the dragoons were still far off, and while the preacher could quickly disappear down into the chimney of Pulpit Rock, the worshippers dispersed in all directions across the hillside, making it very difficult for the soldiers to catch any of them. The Covenanters were so well prepared that even the communion vessels used at these illicit hill-side services were specially prefabricated so that one worshipper could hide the bowl of the communal cup beneath his cloak while others raced off with the stem and base stashed below their jackets, thus denying the pursuing redcoats of any proof that the law had been broken.

As staunch Presbyterians, it's difficult to know what the Covenanters may have felt about Milton's ancient drinking howff, Jean McAlpine's Inn. Named after its original landlady, the historic inn was one of the original hostelries patronised by the cattle drovers when they stopped to enjoy a drink, while they rested the cattle which they drove from the Highlands to the Lowland markets. Sadly it is no longer possible to purchase a drink at Jean McAlpine's, because although the old building still stands, it has long been converted into a private house. A few years ago there was an attempt to redevelop it as a tourist attraction, but this was thwarted by lack of car parking at Milton, where the road is hazardous because of a sharp bend.

Where the path enters the forest, however, there is a small car park where walkers may leave their vehicles. Within yards of its start the walk from the car park at Milton reveals the most stunning views of the start of Loch Ard, which means the Loch of the Height or the High Loch. On the far side, where the road curves tightly round the shore, are many large and prosperous villas, and while he was Secretary of State for Scotland under the Conservative Government of the 1980s, Sir Michael Forsyth chose this delightfully peaceful backwater as his country home. From this point on the footpath there are particularly good views of Dundarroch Mansion, with its little boathouse set picturesquely on the water's edge. It is a scene begging to have been painted by Monet.

This narrow stretch of Loch Ard looks more like a river and would surely also have made a perfect setting for the *Wind In The Willows* if its Edinburgh-born author, Kenneth Grahame, whose family as a cadet branch of the Dukes of Montrose and descendants of the Earls of Menteith were related to the Grahams of Duchray, had chosen to give his classic children's novel a Scottish setting rather than placing it on the Thames. Imagine a tartan-clad Toad hurtling in his vintage car along the Loch Ard Road, perhaps at the same time trying to play the bagpipes. The mind simply boggles!

In the *Wind In The Willows*, Toad's wise old friend Ratty was, of course, not a rat at all but really a water vole, and while in Scotland they are now almost an endangered species, the Great Forest of Loch Ard is still home to some of these interesting little creatures thanks to its many stretches of water, ranging

The old mill building at Milton has been converted into a private house. The massive iron watermill wheel can still be seen. (Arthur Down)

from the impressively large Loch Ard, which broadens out into the distance at this point, to tiny Clashmore Loch deep in the heart of the woods. Two important rivers also flow through the length of the forest: the Duchray Water, which as previously mentioned merges with the Avondhu just to the east of Milton to form the Forth, and the Keltie Water, which later becomes one of that river's tributaries. Forest Enterprise follows very strict guidelines aimed at improving water quality. Work is now proceeding in the Great Forest to clear the banks of its rivers and streams of conifers to allow more light to reach their waters, thus improving conditions for the wildlife living there. Gradually corridors of broadleaved trees and shrubs such as alder, birch, goat willow, hazel, oak and rowan will reach far into the forest, not in rigid straight lines, but like long green fingers, colonising these cleared riverbanks. Hopefully this will make them attractive places for the voles and other wildlife to breed.

At the same time as these improvements have been made, the variety of conifers has also been increased. There are now seventeen different kinds, including Sitka spruce, Norway spruce, Serbian spruce, Scots pine, lodgepole pine, mountain pine, Corsican pine, Douglas fir, noble fir, grand fir, silver fir, European and Japanese larch, hybrid larch, western red cedar, Japanese red cedar and Lawson cypress.

Ecologically friendly schemes such as these to plant a greater variety of trees and thus improve the environment should encourage even more varieties of wildlife to flourish in the Great Forest. Even now, if you are very patient and lucky, it is possible to spot red and roe deer and even some of Scotland's few remaining red squirrels, which have managed to survive the advance of the larger and more aggressive greys. While all of these mammals exist in the Great Forest, the form of wildlife most likely to be seen by the majority of visitors is its birds. In this part of the forest they include the famous capercaillie, blackcock, woodpeckers and barn owls. With the popularity of the computer-animated feature films *Antz* and Walt Disney's *A Bug's Life*, it is perhaps also worth making special mention that the forest in this area is a very good place to watch wood ants at work and to look out for the perfectly formed paper nests of the wood wasps. Hopefully these films may lead children to take a more informed interest in the insect life of the forest.

Walking on west, the footpath allows a brief view of the part of Loch Ard known as The Narrows before it delves deeper into the trees to cut across the headland opposite Dun Dubh, the Black Rock. By the time the path returns to the water's edge, Loch Ard has broadened out and the view across to the north shore includes Helen's Rock, which lies to the right, just before the boathouse.

The path then again leaves the lochside and again cuts off this headland before returning briefly to the shore of a little sheltered inlet. From here it turns inland for the homeward stretch. Much deeper in the forest to the south, and not visible from the path, are situated Duchray House and Duchray Castle. Nearby is Duchray Cottage, better known by its old name of the Bell House. It got this unusual name because its original occupant was an employee of the Glasgow Water Board and the house contained a set of bells which rang to warn him of any problems along the route followed by the water which flowed from Loch Katrine to Mugdock Reservoir at Milngavie. The old-fashioned set of bells can still be seen preserved in one of the outhouses. Beyond the Bell House is the only bridge across the river Duchray and it leads to one of the aqueducts constructed as part of the water scheme. Like all of the other aqueducts and tunnels constructed along the 25¼-mile route, its ruggedly crafted stonework is a tribute to the skill of the Victorian masons who constructed it.

Lack of bridges across the river Duchray also led one of the other cottages in the forest to have another oddity linked with it. At Craigie Cottage there is a high wire across the river and in past years there used to be a wooden bucket attached to it and it was with this strange contraption that the children of the house used to travel at the start and finish of their journeys to school each day. Craigie Cottage is now occupied by more children than ever before, because, rather appropriately, it has been converted into a small local education authority-run outdoor adventure centre. The carving of a bird on one of the stones of the gable wall of the cottage brings to mind the verse penned by Scottish poet William Glen, when he wrote, 'A wee bird cam' to oor ha' door'.

About halfway between the forest footpath and Duchray House, Castle and Cottage, lies Lochan a' Ghleannain and it can be seen from one of the bicycle touring routes through the forest, which runs along its northern shore. The start of the cycle route, like that of the walk, is at Milton and that is also where the entrance to the private forest road leading to five of the Great Forest's youth camp sites, which occupy well-spaced, sheltered settings along the sides of the Duchray Water, is situated. Use of these campsites is limited to organised youth groups.

While the forest road to the youth camps is not open to the public, there are two other way-marked walks which pass close to the shores of the Avondhu, but, rather confusingly, access to these routes is not from Milton but from back in Aberfoyle, from the road past the Covenanters Inn. Both of these trails give views of another of the Great Forest of Loch Ard's water attractions, pretty little Lochan Spling, along both of whose northern and southern shores they stretch. Like the walk from Milton along the southern shore of Loch Ard, the shorter of the two walks from the Covenanters Inn is 3¾ miles long and both of these routes take about two and a half hours to complete. The other forest walk starting from the Covenanters involves a trek of 5½ miles and requires about three and a half hours to walk at a steady comfortable pace.

On the subject of walks in the Great Forest of Loch Ard, it is worth noting that there are two other shorter strolls at its eastern end. Both start from Forest Enterprise's camping and caravan site on the shores of the river Forth at Cobbleland, to the south-east of Aberfoyle. The shorter of the two is three quarters of a mile long and runs along the shore of the river. The other is double that length and climbs the slopes of Doon or Fairy Hill, whose story is covered in chapter seven.

After these walks, the Trossachs Inn, which is situated near the entrance to Cobbleland, is a pleasant retreat in which to relax and enjoy refreshment. It is a popular place with the many campers from Cobbleland and also with those who enjoy staying at the privately operated, award-winning Trossachs Holiday Park on the opposite side of the A81. The Trossachs Inn has a lot of character. It is famed for the colourful personality of its landlord, the poems which he writes about life as it affects the inn and his extensive range of malts. For better or 'verse', it is generally agreed that the quality of his whiskies, which line the gantry of the bar, is much superior to that of the lengthy stanzas which adorn the surrounding walls.

Amongst the malts available to sample at the inn is that produced nearest to it at Glengoyne Distillery, situated only fifteen minutes drive to the south on the A81 road in Blane Valley. Glengoyne is described as the finest and most popular of Scotland's unpeated malt whiskies, 'made using traditional methods to allow an appreciation of all of its subtleties'. Glengoyne first came into production as long ago as 1833, four years before Queen Victoria came to the throne. Conducted tours of its attractive nineteenth-century white-walled buildings, whose grey slate roofs are crowned by its golden pagoda tower, are available all year round apart from Christmas and New Year and each visit concludes with a tasting session. For those really interested in Scottish malts, however, make a point of booking well ahead for one of Glengoyne's tutored nosing sessions held regularly on Wednesday evenings, which allow guests to get to know Scottish malt whisky in the far greater detail which such a fine product deserves.

Back up the road, the Trossachs Inn provides a warm hideaway on a winter night to appreciate a dram, but it is perhaps even pleasanter on the long light nights of summer, for it is set right on the shores of the Forth and, on warm evenings, it is also possible to wine and dine outdoors at tables overlooking the river. The Trossachs Inn is indeed one of the few places that this pleasure can be enjoyed along the full length of the course of the Forth on its way to the North Sea.

After this hopefully worthwhile diversion to explore the other forest paths and the delights of dining alfresco at the old Trossachs Inn, it is now time to hasten back to the other side of Aberfoyle, to Milton, to pick up the route to Inversnaid. There, overlooking the road at Milton, the little old letterbox set into the wall is an interesting reminder that an excellent way to make this journey is by the wee red post bus, which operates a regular service every day except Sunday. Since 1968 it has been possible to use the Royal Mail to deliver yourself as well as your letters and parcels, thanks to the introduction of the post buses. These are scarlet-liveried minibuses, which carry up to fourteen passengers as well as the mail. They have proved so popular that there are now more then 120 post bus routes in all parts of rural Scotland, including three in the Trossachs. One post bus runs from Callander post office and delivers both mail and passengers to Invertrossachs, Kilmahog, Garthonzie, the other Milton on the shores of Loch Venachar, Brig O'Turk, An Taigh Mor Timeshare Development, the Achray Hotel, the Trossachs Pier on Loch Katrine, the Forest Centre, Aberfoyle, the Rob Roy Motel and Port of Menteith. The other two post buses are based at the post office in Main Street in Aberfoyle and both serve this route along the shores of

Aberfoyle from the car park.
(William F. Hendrie)

The post office in Aberfoyle is the base for the two post buses which deliver both mail and passengers along the road through Strathard to Inversnaid on Loch Lomond and Stronachlachar on Loch Katrine.
(William F. Hendrie)

Loch Ard, one travelling every weekday as far as Kinlochard and the other continuing all the way to Stronachlachar and Inversnaid. All three of these post buses are timed to connect with Midland Scottish First Bus services at Aberfoyle and Callander and with the morning sailing of the *Sir Walter Scott*, which sails from Trossachs Pier to Stronachlachar, thus making them a very valuable asset to visitors to the district as well as local residents.

After Milton, the post bus makes its next pickup at the Glassart, or Glassert as it is sometimes spelt. This local beauty spot was a favourite destination for Aberfoyle Sunday school picnics in the early years of the twentieth century, with the pupils and their teachers and the minister all travelling out to it on open hay carts to enjoy an afternoon of food and fun. The annual outing to Glassart was the reward for regular weekly attendance at Sunday school and bible class and it is said that on this occasion even the minister relaxed and unbuttoned his dog collar.

The farmstead at Ledart overlooks Loch Ard, whose name means the Loch of the Heights. (Fergus Wood)

From Glassart the post bus drives on to the Altskeith Hotel and Ledart Farm. Ledart is the home of the enterprising Fergus Wood, the enthusiastic sheep farmer whose brainchild, the Scottish Wool Centre in Aberfoyle, is the Trossach's largest tourist attraction. Built with the backing of the Scottish Tourist Board it has been a resounding success, and, while some villagers feared that it might harm trade in the existing shops along Main Street, it is now generally agreed to have given the area's tourist trade a tremendous boost.

Devoted to telling the story of wool, from the sheep's back to the fashion catwalk, the stars of the show at the Scottish Wool Centre are the sheep them-selves as they take the stage in the centre's 150-seat theatre. And in a new event for 2004 seven different types of sheepdog show their prowess in performances three times each day in the canine 'fame academy'. American guests are often the most intrigued to find out more about the sheep, as they are a comparatively uncommon animal in most parts of the USA. Many also buy little pottery minia-tures of ewes, rams and lambs as souvenirs of their transatlantic visit to Scotland, and from the number sold it appears that quite a few American homes boast signs beside the front door adorned with lambs and that classic Glaswegian greeting, 'Ewes welcome!'

The idea for the Scottish Wool Centre all began when farmer Fergus agreed to allow some groups of pupils from Dounans Outdoor Centre to come to see his own sheep on the farm at Ledart. Now, at the purpose-built centre which opened in 1992 on the site of the former railway station in Aberfoyle, there are many more breeds of sheep to be seen. First on stage is the Soay with its horns and short dark fleece. By tradition, its wool is plucked between the finger and thumb when it becomes loose during the early summer months. It is followed by three more sheep from the islands, the multi-horned Hebridean, the Boreray, from the little island of that name in the St Kilda group, and the Shetland, which has the finest fleece of any Scottish sheep. All four are a reminder of what sheep used to look like before the Romans introduced into this country what became our modern woolly sheep, such as the next two performers, the Scottish black-face and the North Country Cheviot, which Sir John Sinclair developed and introduced into Caithness in the 1790s. Last of the sheep to parade is the largest, the merino, introduced into Spain by the Muslim Moors in AD 711. With merinos from Australia and blackfaces from Scotland, it is too tempting not to choose this appropriate setting to pose the old joke: What do you get if you cross a sheep with a kangaroo? Woolly jumpers, of course!

Although the merino is the final sheep to appear, it is not the end of the show, because Fergus has also always bred Cashmere goats at Ledart and they provide the finale, with the commentary from one of Mr Wood's shepherds telling the audience that cashmere is the most expensive animal fibre in the world, currently worth fifty times the value of best-quality merino wool. Most popular of all the animal performers at the Scottish Wool Centre is, however, the farm collie, who is happy to shake paws with the audience at the end of the performance. The most famous of the sheepdogs is Dorothy, the only dog in the country to be presented with a 'Welcome Host' certificate by the Scottish Tourist Board because of the way she always greeted visitors. Now the elderly Dorothy enjoys her retirement snoozing in her basket, but still delighted to be petted by the passing tourists.

For the younger, active dogs, sheepdog trials are held at regular intervals at the centre at weekends during the summer season and there are also displays of how the dogs are trained for their duties in the hills. Sheep shearing demonstrations also draw the crowds. These events take place in the field in front of the centre, while indoors there are spinning and weaving demonstrations.

The Scottish Wool Centre at Aberfoyle is the headquarters for the worldwide Back-to-Back competition which is held every year during the first weekend in

Iain Grant, Chairman of the Scottish Tourist Board, presents sheepdog Dorothy with her Welcome Host Certificate at the Scottish Wool Centre, Aberfoyle, as her proud master, Fergus Wood, looks on. (Scottish Wool Centre, Aberfoyle)

June. At the centre teams of seven, comprising shearers, spinners and knitters from all over Great Britain, compete to see who can be fastest to produce a sweater from the minute the fleece is removed from the sheep's back to the moment when a model pulls the finished garment over her shoulders and onto her back. During the same twenty-four hour period, similar competitions are held in Canada, Australia and New Zealand and the fastest time achieved is declared the winner. At present the record is held by a Scottish team from the Islesburgh Centre in Lerwick in the Shetland Islands, who completed their model's jumper in only five hours and seventeen minutes. The ladies in the home team representing Aberfoyle include founder members Ann Duke and Ann Simpson, together with Lynn Carvana, Lorna Malarky and Chrissie-Ann Owens.

The Scottish Wool Centre also has many other facilities, including a children's petting farm, where they can meet the sheep and goats and bottle-feed the lambs, and a rural-style self-service restaurant and café from whose tables visitors can enjoy views out over the river Forth as it flows by. There is also a large shopping area offering a vast range of Scottish knitwear, tweed garments and other clothing, Scottish food and novelty items ranging from tartan travel rugs to tartan tea cosies. The latter prove a great novelty with American visitors, who, believing that the correct way to make a good cup of tea is to dip a teabag, like a drowned rat, in a mug of lukewarm water, take a lot of convincing of the existence of teapots, even more so tartan cosies to keep them warm. They are indeed often firmly of the opinion that the tea cosies are as mythical as the little haggis, with its two outside legs longer than those on the inside so that it can run the more easily round the slopes of local hillsides, and declare that they know for sure that the tea cosies are really tartan bonnets probably worn as protection against the infamous Trossachs midges, with the slot for the spout really a way to poke out one's nose for a quick breath of air before the wee airborne menaces are able to bite!

On the shores of Loch Ard the combination of water and trees seems to attract even more midges and visitors often ponder why the Lord ever created these little pests. It seems, however, that all God's creatures do have a purpose and that this even includes the Trossachs midges, because local farmers confirm that by biting the cows and sheep, they drive the beasts to try to escape by climbing up the hillside, thus giving fresh grass the chance to grow at the foot of the glens. Like mosquitoes in tropical countries, it is only the female midge which bites to obtain the blood needed for reproduction. The problem, of course, is how to identify the females of the species as they swoop down in swirling black clouds to the terror especially of the campers and other outdoor types, who are sure that the Trossachs midges are definitely related to Dracula and are truly mini vampires who regard them as human blood banks! Local tips for minimising the menace of the midges include smoking the filthiest-smelling pipe tobacco and using oil of citronella in preference to buying the costly branded insect repellents. It is also possible nowadays to purchase an electronic device which emits a very high-pitched tone, which is said to deter the midges from coming near.

Loch Ard.

Even if the midges are in the air, a climb up the farm path beside Ledart Farm is worthwhile to visit the waterfall and to find Helen's Pool, the deep, dark pool on the hillside near where location shooting took place for the film version of *Rob Roy* starring Richard Todd, although better known nowadays is the latest version starring Irish actor Liam Neeson.

Aberfoyle has also been used for location shooting for several other big-screen films, including a spectacular, blazing, hillside helicopter crash in one of the early James Bond movies and *Geordie*, starring Bill Travers as the wee laddie who grew up to become a caber-tossing star of the Highland Games and the Melbourne Olympic Games. On television it has been seen in the series *Tinker, Tailor, Soldier, Spy* as well as *Dr Finlay's Casebook*.

A short distance further along the shore of Loch Ard is the watersports centre for the Forest Hills Lochside Resort, whose luxury apartments overlook its calm waters. The heart of this very successful, popular timeshare development, which was built by Barrett, is still the charming rather old world Forest Hills Hotel, operated by Scotland's largest hotel chain, MacDonald Hotels. It has all of the facilities of a deluxe resort, including an indoor swimming pool and an ice rink for curling in winter and indoor carpet bowls during the summer months. The Forest Hills watersports centre means the sails of dinghies often bring a splash of colour to Loch Ard, on whose waters the boats of trout fishers are also often seen. Sailboarding, windsurfing, canoeing and kayaking are also available.

From the little pier at Forest Hills, there is a view of Eilean Gorm, which translated from the Gaelic means the Blue Island, which lies at the entrance to the bay on the far side of the loch. On the south side of the road at the far end of the loch is the entrance to one of the cycle tracks though the forest and it is possible to ride all the way through the woods to Kirkton of Aberfoyle.

At the far end of the loch is also the hamlet of Kinlochard, whose name is Gaelic for the Head of Loch of the Height. Set in the heart of Strathard, it is a peaceful little place, whose sub-post office is one of the timetabled stops for the post bus. While the post office is still open for business, sadly the village school was closed by Stirling Council in June 1998, despite a strenuous fight by local parents and most members of the little community. The closure means that the pupils now have to travel every morning to Aberfoyle Primary. While the children have been warmly welcomed to the school and settled in well, it is sad that Kinlochard has been deprived of this focal point for its community life.

On the royal journey to Inversnaid, Queen Victoria's coach was halted at Kinlochard so that Her Majesty might alight to stroll on the lochside and, delighted with the view of Ben Lomond, she made a drawing of it in her sketchbook.

It is intriguing to wonder if any of the courtiers who escorted the queen on her travels through the Trossachs dared tell Her Majesty how the next place of interest along the route got its name. It is a very old croft called the Teapot, which seems a rather odd but quite innocuous title until it is revealed that this was really a way of disguising from the authorities the fact that the refreshment which its owners dispensed for a small fee to passing travellers, was somewhat more potent than the tea which they advertised. For the Teapot was really a cover for an illicit still, where the crofter produced a well-above-proof whisky, drams of which he did indeed pour from an old china teapot. Rough compared with the smooth malt produced at Glengoyne, the Teapot's brew nonetheless soon gained such a reputation for its potency that it was even sold in Glasgow. Perhaps because of the intoxicating effects of its 'moonshine' whisky, the old Teapot Farm was also the scene of many appearances by fairies, brownies, kelpies and other wee folk!

The real name for the Teapot is Bullburn Cottage, but that seems to have been forgotten, for it is shown by its nickname on many maps.

Shortly after the Teapot, the road passes Blairuskinmore and then on the left is the entrance to the forest walk, which crosses the breadth of the forest before skirting the southern slopes of Ben Lomond to join up with the famous long-distance walking route the West Highland Way at Rowardennan on the east shore of Loch Lomond. Beware, however, that it is a considerable hike from this point on the road to Inversnaid to reach Loch Lomond, before you even start tackling the West Highland Way. It is also possible at this point to climb Ben Lomond from this side by taking the route past Comer Farm. From there it is a steep climb and most walkers prefer the easier method of climbing it from the car park at Balmaha, from where there is a well-worn path to the summit.

The road next skirts little Loch Dhu, which translated from the Gaelic means the Black Lake, and the longer and larger Loch Chon. Loch Chon, translated,

Distinctive black and white-painted iron milestones such as this one were specially erected along the royal route followed by Queen Victoria and Prince Albert when they travelled this way at the opening of the Loch Katrine Waterworks in October 1859. This one is on the route between Aberfoyle and Inversnaid and Stronachlachar, the latter place name being given preference as it was from there that Her Majesty travelled after performing the official ceremony by opening the sluices, which can still be seen beside Royal Cottage on the shores of Loch Katrine. (Arthur Down)

means the Lake of the Dog, but today it is for its trout that it is famed, with good angling available by permit on its waters. There is a car park at the southern end of Loch Chon, beyond which the road hugs the shore. On the other side the trees of the forest come right down to the roadside, making this one of the most ruggedly attractive of the drives through the Trossachs. When weather conditions have been really wet and wild the views across Loch Chon take on an added interest because it is then that it is possible to see at their best the Pig Foot Waterfalls. When in spate, they send a torrent of water 1,000ft down into the loch, but in dry conditions they practically disappear. Completing the picture, motoring north and looking across the waters of Loch Chon to its far end, the eye is caught by the white walls of Frenich Farm. Up on the hillside to the north-west of Frenich, hidden by the trees of the forest, lies tiny Lochan Mhiam nan Carn.

Continuing on beyond Frenich the road runs through the forest until it emerges above Loch Arklet. At the north-eastern corner of the loch the road divides. One fork descends to Stronachlachar on the shore of Loch Katrine while the other follows the north shore of Loch Arklet to Inversnaid on Loch Lomond. Like Loch Katrine, Loch Arklet has been incorporated into the scheme to supply Glasgow with its fresh water supply. From Loch Arklet the water flows through a feeder pipe and then down a cascade into Loch Katrine.

As a result of it being a reservoir, building along the shores of Loch Arklet has been discouraged and they are therefore almost deserted apart from the few buildings at Corriearklet and a short way further on at the entrance to Glen Arklet.

After the end of Loch Arklet, where the road crosses the Snaid Burn, there is an excellent viewpoint from which to look out over the northern stretch of Loch Lomond and across to the Arrocher Alps and the other high mountains of Argyll, including the famous Cobbler. Soon after the viewpoint, the road drops dramatically to the shore of Loch Lomond at Inversnaid with its hotel and pier.

For many years the hotel was run by well-known local farmer George Buchan and it continued to flourish under its new owner, English hotelier Michael Wells. The very enterprising Mr Wells breathed life into tourism in this part of Scotland by developing a chain of hotels, including the Loch Achray and the Arrocher Hotel on Loch Long, and filling them regularly by organising his own bus tours. Mr Wells clearly identified a niche in the holiday market, especially amongst older visitors, for well-organised week-long residential tours, which combine value for money with good food, comfortable surroundings and something to do in the evenings, including Highland and Scottish dancing displays and lively ceilidhs in which guests are encouraged to participate. Inversnaid Pier used to be a port of call for the largest of Scotland's inland loch steamers, the appropriately named *Maid of the Loch*, and was, during her latter years of operation, her northern terminus. Originally part of the Calmac fleet, the beautiful white-hulled, 750-passenger *Maid*, which was the last paddle steamer built in Britain, was a costly vessel to operate with a ship's company of thirty-three to pay. Despite local authority subsidies it proved impossible to make her pay and she was withdrawn from service before being sold to Alloa Breweries. The brewery owners had ambitious plans to use her both for daytime cruises on the loch and as a floating restaurant moored alongside the pier at Balloch, where guests could enjoy dinner with a view in the evening.

For a short time the future for the *Maid* looked promising and Alloa Breweries also purchased a second vessel, the well-known MV *Countess of Breadalbane*, which had formerly operated at different periods both on the river Clyde and on Loch Awe. For her new career on Loch Lomond, Alloa Breweries renamed her *Countess Fiona*. With a crew of only six and a passenger capacity of about 160, the little *Countess* proved much more economical to operate and for several seasons Alloa Breweries provided a service on the loch using her, including regular calls at Inversnaid. Unfortunately, however, they failed to make a success of reintroducing the *Maid of the Loch* and in the end abandoned the effort, at the same time withdrawing *Countess Fiona*, which has since been broken up.

After a succession of equally unsuccessful owners, the *Maid of the Loch* was left to deteriorate for over a decade at Balloch, but now there is happier news as she has been acquired by Dumbarton Council and a charitable body called the Loch Lomond Steamship Co. has been founded to try to ensure this unique asset again helps to boost tourism on Loch Lomond. Smartly repainted down to the waterline, the enthusiastic charity members have involved students from Glasgow's Anniesland College of Further Education to help them to restore the interior of the vessel to her former glory, so hopefully the *Maid of the Loch* will once again set sail on Loch Lomond and include the pier at Inversnaid as one of her regular ports of call.

In the meantime Inversnaid is still well worth visiting, by the 14-mile-long landward route from Aberfoyle, to see amongst other attractions the spectacular Snaid Falls. William Wordsworth visited the Snaid Falls while on his tour of the Trossachs with his sister Dorothy. As he was admiring the rushing, tumbling waters of the falls, it is said that his eye also caught sight of a bonnie local lass and that she inspired his poem 'Sweet Highland Girl'. The Trossachs gave Wordsworth much to write about, because his poem 'The Solitary Reaper' is claimed to have been composed after his visit to the Braes of Balquhidder.

Today there are few lassies, or for that matter laddies, resident in Inversnaid, but although it has less than a handful of pupils, the little single-teacher village school is still open, because the 28-mile roundtrip to Aberfoyle each day was deemed too long, and in winter too dangerous, for such young children. Other children also come regularly to Inversnaid, because the former village kirk was converted in 1991 into an outdoor adventure centre operated by the Glasgow Battalion of the Boys' Brigade. This little kirk was built in 1895 and was known as a mission church. During the final years when it was still used for worship, the minister travelled to it by boat across Loch Lomond. But before then however the kirk had its own minister and the manse can still be seen. It must have been one of the most unusual manses in Scotland, not just because of its remote situation, but because it is built of corrugated iron.

Another interesting place at Inversnaid is Garrison Farm, because it is still possible to see one of the old walls of the fort built to house the redcoat dragoons from whose regiment it acquired its name. Garrison Farm is also a reminder of the fact that the route between Aberfoyle and Inversnaid was built originally as a military road, so that the fort could be kept supplied while its soldiers tried to bring some law and order to the area. One of the outlaws whom they tried to capture was Rob Roy and one of the caves in which he hid to escape them is situated near Inversnaid on the West Highland Way.

From Inversnaid there is a choice of walks along this, Scotland's most famous long-distance walking route. To the south the well-worn path skirts the shore of the loch and passes through the Lomondside Oakwoodlands to reach Rowardennan, where the Scottish Youth Hostel Association has one of its most attractive and very popular properties. The building was formerly one of the Duke of Montrose's hunting lodges, where parties of his guests stayed during the shooting season.

Turning in the other direction, the West Highland Way continues along the northern shores of Loch Lomond, past the Hill of Doon and Ardleish, with its views out to the little island of Ivow. This is one of the last places in Scotland where wild goats still forage. They usually live on the higher slopes of the surrounding hills, as they can somehow find enough to eat where not even the sturdiest sheep can survive. Occasionally they come further down and are spotted by walkers, who usually smell them before they see them!

Beyond the far end of Loch Lomond, the West Highland Way continues through Glen Falloch to Crianlarich. From here there is the option of walking its entire length to Fort William and Ben Nevis, the Heavenly Hill, which at 4,406ft is not only Scotland's highest mountain, but the highest in Great Britain.

chapter nine

Scotland's only Lake?

While the Trossachs cannot lay claim to Scotland's highest mountain, having indeed to be content with only one Munro in the form of shapely 3,192ft-high Ben Lomond, it *can* boast to being home to the country's only lake.

The title 'Scotland's only lake' is not, however, a strictly accurate description of the Lake of Menteith, which lies on the eastern edge of the Trossachs between Aberfoyle and Thornhill. There are in fact several other small lakes in various parts of Scotland, but Menteith is definitely by far the largest and best known. Why this beautiful stretch of water, in the middle of which is situated the island of Inchmahome with its picturesque ruined priory, bears this anglicised title, is an unsolved mystery. Perhaps the most probable explanation is that the area was first mapped by an English cartographer and he simply did not know any better.

It is interesting to ponder whether it was the term 'Lake of Menteith' on early maps which led to the Trossachs sometimes being described in Victorian times as Scotland's Lake District. Thankfully, however, the shores of Menteith are nothing like as crowded as those of Windermere or Derwent Water and it remains a delightful rural retreat, virtually untouched by commercialisation.

The almost circular-shaped lake has a circumference of approximately 5 miles. It is 2 miles long from east to west and at its widest is 1½ miles from north to south. At its deepest it reaches 80ft. In appearance it is very different from lochs of the Trossachs. The Victorian guidebook sums up the difference thus:

> The shores of the Lake of Menteith exhibit none of the grandeur and wild magnificence of most Highland loch scenery, but present charming pictures, in which soft pastoral beauty is co-mingled with rich sylvan luxuriance. Its banks and the three islands, which bedeck its pellucid surface, are covered with magnificent old trees, which are survivors of those which adorned the park of the Earls of Menteith, enriched with the soft feathery tangle of murmuring reeds. The whole scene, especially on a calm summer evening, when the sunlight gilds the neighbouring slopes of the Menteith Hills and casts its declining rays through the intervening foliage

Canoeing on the Lake of Menteith, with the slopes of the Menteith Hills in the background. (Scott Guthrie Pollock)

across the placid lake and over its islands with their trees and ruins, is one calculated to produce in the contemplative mind, reflections as calm and quiet as those in the lake's transparent waters.

Nowadays the lake is still as beautifully unspoilt and its wildlife is so rich and varied that it has been designated a Site of Special Scientific Interest, and this classification will guarantee its protection from any threat of development in the future. Most interesting of the many species of birds to be found around the lake are the ospreys. Local people have known about the presence of these magnificent sea hawks for many years, but thankfully it has never been publicised in the way which it has been at Boat of Garten on Speyside, and the many fishermen who enjoy their sport here regard spotting one of the ospreys catching a trout in its talons not as a threat but as a bonus to their day on the water.

The fishing enthusiasts can indeed afford to be so magnanimous about the osprey's catch, because they know that the waters of Menteith are so well managed and so well regularly stocked that they are themselves often able to reach the daily fishing limit of fifteen trout to a boat, so why grudge the sea hawk its tea?! Before the lake became an established trout fishery, it was also famous for another kind of wildlife: huge pike. These scavenger fish, with their rows of sharp teeth, grew fatter by snatching ducklings and other small birds from the surface of the lake. Pike caught on Menteith often weighed as much as 17lbs and resembled the monster fish which south sea island natives always seemed to be carving up into steaks in comics such as the *Beano* and *Dandy*.

There has been a fishery at the Lake of Menteith since the 1920s and the company which at present looks after its waters, Lake of Menteith Fisheries Ltd, was established over twenty-five years ago. Its principal objectives are to preserve its amenity and to provide top-class angling for both club and individual fishing enthusiasts. Fly-fishing is from boats, all of which are 15-footers fitted with 3.3hp mariner outboard engines. With over 700 acres of fishing water to cover, the outboard motors are almost essential, while individual fishermen can also bring their own craft so long as they do not exceed 4hp.

Each year the fishing season on Menteith starts early at the beginning of April and continues right through until 1 November, and, during the main summer months, it is stocked with 1,000 fish every week to ensure good sport. The lake is indeed so well known for the challenge which it offers that it attracts keen anglers from all over Scotland and the north of England to do battle against robust Rainbows and beautiful Brownies. When they are released the fish weigh an average of 1½lbs, but the feeding in the waters of Menteith is so plentiful that by the time they are caught many top 3lbs. The records for the heaviest fish caught on Menteith are currently held by a wild Brownie, weighed in at 5.5lbs, and by a Rainbow, which reached an impressive 12lbs.

The Lake of Menteith Fisheries Ltd's modern lodge is unobtrusively situated on the north-eastern shores of the lake at what is known as Hotel Bay, handily close to the historic Lake Hotel from which this corner takes its name. The lodge is well equipped and its facilities are designed to cater for disabled anglers. Once fishing is over for the day and they've weighed in, the bar at the nearby hotel makes a fine comfortable setting to recount tales of record catches and also stories of the fish which got away, to lure anglers back for future days of bliss on the lake.

As well as being popular with fishermen, the Lake Hotel is also a favourite with those who like to enjoy afternoon tea with a view, and many will recall that this scene was well known on television screens when several episodes of the much-loved original version of A.J. Cronin's *Dr Finlay's Casebook*, with its familiar theme music of Duncan's March from the Little Suite, were filmed here. The star of the BBC series, Bill Simpson, fell so much in love with the place that he returned there for his wedding, and more recently well-known Scottish television personalities Viv Lumsden and Allan Douglas also chose Port of Menteith kirk and the hotel with its beautiful grounds for their marriage.

Nearby, other features of interest include the mausoleum of the Grahams of Gartmore and the old kirk. The kirk was built in Gothic style in 1878. It has a congregation of about a hundred drawn from the area around Port of Menteith. This small congregation is able to survive and continue worshipping in the setting of their lovely Victorian kirk by being linked with the parish church in Aberfoyle. This means that the two kirks are served by the one minister, but retain their independence by still having their own elders, sessions and boards of management. The minister resides at the manse on Loch Ard Road in Aberfoyle and the old nineteenth-century whitewashed manse beside the kirk at Port of Menteith has become a privately owned home. Beautifully situated overlooking the lake, the gateposts at the end of the driveway leading up to it from the main road are worth stopping to look at as they are of a most unusual design consisting of wrought iron enclosed in stone.

Port of Menteith, which was once a burgh of Barony, still possesses its village school, which is housed in modern premises at the road junction. A short distance further south, Port of Menteith is also home to another of the Trossachs'

The Lake of Menteith ferryman in the 1960s. (Scott Guthrie Pollock)

outdoor youth centres, the Boyd Centre at Dykehead. The attractively designed centre is based around an old stone-built, whitewashed, slate-roofed farmhouse and its adjoining farm steading, which is spread round a sheltered courtyard. It is named in honour of Willie Boyd, a pioneer of the Scottish Schoolboys Club in Glasgow which operates it. Willie and members of his family have given over eighty years of service to this very worthwhile organisation. The centre provides self-catering accommodation for parties of up to thirty-six participants. It is particularly suitable for school parties and youth and community groups. There are six comfortable dormitories for the youngsters and bedrooms for staff members, while other accommodation includes a dining room, lounge and games room. The Boyd Centre is suitable for visitors who are disabled.

From this, the most visited part of the lake, which also includes the pier from where the motor launches of Historic Scotland provide a ferry service to and from the Priory of Inchmahome, which is described later, we move on first to look at other geographic features of its shores. First, in a clockwise direction, comes the long stretch known as Rednock Shore, which runs south to a little nose of land where an early chapel is believed to have overlooked the lake. Round the other side of this wee headland lies Kate's Brae and round the next headland to the south, where the gravel pit is situated, the lake opens out into Lochend Bay. Lochend House stands overlooking the lake and from it a track leads past Lochend Farm to the main road north to Port of Menteith and south to Arnprior. As its name suggests, Lochend Bay marks the southern extremity of the lake. On the south shore running west, it is separated from Otter Bay by the little protrusion of the Bogle Knowe, which roughly translated means the Ghost Hill, yet another intriguing link to the area's connections with the supernatural.

On the far side of Bogle Knowe, the little inlet called Tod Hole, the Fox's Lair, is another indication of the abundance of wildlife around the shores of the lake. To the south lies the flat land of Cardross Moss, with, on its far side, the remains of an ancient prehistoric crannog settlement. Further round Menteith, the west bank of Otter Bay is formed by the most prominent of the geographic features of the lake shore, a peninsula which runs north, pointing towards Inchmahome, inch being the Gaelic for an island. Round the other side of this narrow peninsula lies Sandy Bay, whose long southern shore is known as the Heronry, where many of these attractive birds, with their long legs and elongated necks, are often sighted.

The outer limits of Sandy Bay are marked by the lake's other two islands. The larger of the two is Inch Talla, which means the Isle of the Hall, and the ruins of the Earls of Menteith's former family castle stronghold, dating from 1427, can be glimpsed through the trees, though landing is not permitted. Landing is also banned on the smaller island whose name, the Isle of Dogs, comes from the fact that it was there that the Menteiths had the kennels for their hunting hounds.

Directly north of little Isle of Dogs and due west of Inch Talla on the west shore of the lake is Stable Point, which is in turn the spot on the mainland where the Earls of Menteith kept the horses which they rode to the hunt. A short distance to the south of the Point the lake is drained by the Malling Burn. It is one of two streams which flow out of the lake. On the other side of Stable Point is Gateside Bay and on its far shore Portend Burn drains out of the lake. After the spot where this second stream pours out of the lake comes Coille Don and thereafter the Portend Shore and the aptly-named Reedy Bay complete the circumnavigation before arrival back at the angler's wooden fishing headquarters at Hotel Bay, where briefing instructions are given before the day's sport and where the weigh-ins take place at the end of what has hopefully been another good day's fishing.

While trout fishing is the sport mainly practised on the Lake of Menteith nowadays, it has also always traditionally been associated with curling, and since the Second World War it has been the scene of that winter sport's greatest competition. The Grand Match, as this event is appropriately known, is played between two teams representing the North of Scotland and the South of Scotland, but, far from taking place annually, this very lively, colourful event can only be held during the severest of winters, when the whole surface of the lake is frozen solid.

During every cold snap the big question is 'Is it bearing?' and originally the rules of curling demanded that Menteith be covered with a sheet of ice no less than 8ins thick before play could be considered. However this has now been increased still further to an even more demanding 10ins of ice! The reason for this is that on the last occasion that a Grand Match Bonspeil was decreed possible on the Lake on 7 February 1979, and 2,000 'ends' successfully played, the crowd which arrived to watch the players compete in this rare event was so large that it was feared that lives were being put at risk. It was estimated that no fewer than 10,000 spectators thronged the ice to watch the curling on that bitterly cold winter day, so popular had this originally Scottish game become, thanks to its development as an international sport, its inclusion as a regular event at the Winter Olympics and its resultant exposure on television.

The Royal Caledonian Curling Club was originally founded in 1838 as the Grand Caledonian Curling Club. It gained its royal title five years later in 1843, but there has only been a World Curling Championship since 1959. While most curling matches now take place indoors on artificial rinks, it is when the sport is played in the open air that it really comes into its own as a truly great spectacle and lives up to its nickname of 'The Roaring Game'. This name comes not from the enthusiastic shouts of the players as they respond to the orders of their skip and sweep or refrain from sweeping, according to his instructions, in order to increase or decrease the friction and pressure on the ice to place the stone in the house, as the target is known. 'The Roaring Game' in fact comes from the rumbling sound, like distant thunder, of the heavy granite stones as they trundle over the ice at outdoor matches.

Modern curling stones are sleek, polished objects, made to a standard size, preferably from the excellent granite from Ailsa Craig, or Paddy's Mile Stone as it is often known, out in the estuary of the river Clyde, but the original stones used in the game, when it was always played outdoors on frozen surfaces like that of Menteith, were simply granite boulders found along the shores of streams, whose running water had over centuries smoothed their rugged edges. Even when the sport was regulated by all of the rules which Scottish lawyers, who were often enthusiastic curlers in Victorian times, could devise, stones still varied in size and shape, as did their iron handles, which were often forged by local blacksmiths and farriers. The style of play also varied greatly from the present day, with one nineteenth-century print showing a curler on a Scottish loch, his stone raised to shoulder level, despite its obvious size and weight, ready to deliver his shot.

Whether the dramatic sounds of The Roaring Game will ever again echo back from the Menteith Hills above the lake during a Grand Match is questionable, for the future of this famous bonspeil seems in grave doubt. The reason for this is that the recent mild winters of the 1990s, allegedly as a result of global warming, have meant that the ice on the lake has for many years never begun to reach anything like the thickness required to allow players and spectators, with their well-filled hipflasks and tartan travelling rugs, to brave the cold and bring the highly enjoyable scenes of old to life again on its frozen surface.

For the statistically minded, however, it is interesting to note that there have been thirty-five Grand Matches played in various parts of Scotland over the past century and a half, thus averaging one such bonspeil approximately every five years. A Grand Match is therefore long overdue. It will be interesting to see what type of weather the winters of the new millennium will bring. It is also encouraging to note that if the required 10ins of ice does ever again form across the surface of Menteith, thus permitting a Grand Match to be held, there is likely to be a demand for a junior bonspeil as well, because whereas in the past curling was a sport for middle-aged and elderly lawyers, ministers and doctors and, in more recent years, their wives, many Scottish teenagers have now discovered the thrills of this historic sport and taken it up as an energetic winter pastime.

In the past when the Lake of Menteith appears to have frozen solid more frequently, the curlers did not have a monopoly of the ice. There are also descriptions of the local young folk from the surrounding villages and farms walking and riding for miles to reach its frozen surface to enjoy the delights of ice skating. Very few of the participants in these outdoor sessions owned proper skates. Undeterred, however, they simply improvised by strapping blades to their ordinary boots. A tent was often set up on the ice at Hotel Bay at Port of Menteith, to act not as a first aid position, but as a refreshment stall. From it glasses of hot whisky toddy were sold to keep both the curlers and skaters warm, so these must have been rather jolly, if perhaps a wee bit dangerous, occasions, with probably all the more need for some first aid to be available!

In addition to curling and skating, there was also a tradition in many parts of Scotland that if any local loch, pond or even dam was frozen on New Year's Day, then the holiday should be the occasion for all of the local youths to gather to play an improvised game of shinty on ice. The Museum of Scotland, in Edinburgh's Chamber Street, has a wonderfully detailed painting by the father of Arthur Conan Doyle, creator of Sherlock Holmes, depicting Scottish youths taking part in just such a shinty-on-ice spectacular. According to Doyle's painting, the shinty match took place amongst the more established winter outdoor pursuits of curling and skating, with the shinty players enthusiastically wielding their sticks, much to the hazard no doubt of all of the other users of the ice.

Whether the monks who inhabited the priory out in the middle of the Lake of Menteith ever joined in any of these winter sports is not recorded, but to this day there is still the garth, the lawn in the centre of the cloisters, where they used to play games of bowls, probably in the style of the popular French sport of boules. Mention of the game of boules conjures up images of warm summer evenings in contrast to the image of Menteith as a frozen winter wonderland, and Inchmahome Priory is indeed very much a place to visit on sunny summer days, when the surrounding island blossoms with bluebells and other wild flowers.

Thanks to its island location, the ancient ruins of the Priory of Inchmahome have been largely protected from vandalism or the theft of their stones and so are much more complete than any monastery on the mainland. Historic Scotland, the present guardians into whose care the Graham family has entrusted the priory, operate two modern motor launches, the *Earl of Menteith* and the *Earl of Mar*, on the short seven-minute crossing from the pier at Port of Menteith. These little vessels, which are each licensed to carry twelve passengers, operate a regular shuttle service to and from the island every day from April until the end of September during standard Historic Scotland opening hours and there is no need to pay the ferryman, as the cost of the trip is included in the price of admission to the priory. At weekends and on holidays the two little craft ply regularly to and from the island, but on quieter days in the middle of the week there is an intriguing signalling system on the end of the little stone pier at Port of Menteith for passengers to use to attract the attention of the ferryman.

While sailing across the usually placid surface of the lake use these few moments to try to imagine that you are travelling way back in time to the early years of the thirteenth century, when the first Augustinian Canons rowed their way from the mainland over to the solitude of their island sanctuary. The buildings whose ruins stand on the island today date back to 1238 when the priory was founded by Walter Comyn, fourth Earl of Menteith. It is believed, however, that there was an even earlier Celtic monastery, dedicated to St Colman, who was known by the monks on Inchmahome as Macholman.

As you step off the ferry and walk up the short stone pier onto the island's grassy shores, turn left and enter the ruins of the priory church by the west door. Like all medieval churches, the one on Inchmahome was built facing east for the religious reason that this meant that worshippers could pray facing towards the birthplace of Jesus in the Holy Land and for the more practical one that as dawn broke the rays of the sun flooded in through the window in the apse to illuminate the high altar situated beneath it, the setting for the first service of the day.

As you walk on into the church, step carefully over the stones of the foundations and look up to the left. There, high above, you will see the remains of the belfry, where the bell once tolled to summon the brothers to worship. Continue on down the length of the pillared nave, which is still impressive in its ruined state. At its far end you will come to the little chancel. Following the Reformation in 1560 and the ending of regular worship in the church, with the abandonment of Catholicism in favour of Protestantism, this part of the building became a burial ground. The skull and crossbones on several of the gravestones do not indicate, as some young visitors would love to believe, that pirates once sailed the waters of the lake; these carvings are simply symbols which, in the Middle Ages, were a very visual way of trying to depict death.

The sculptured stone effigies of the Earl and Countess of Menteith in the chapter house of the Priory of Inchmahome. The island's name means the peaceful island. (Arthur Down)

Of particular interest amongst the moss-covered tombstones are the much more recent ones of the famous Don Roberto – Robert Bontine Cunninghame Graham – and his wife Gabrielle, the story of whose colourful life together in both Victorian and Edwardian Scotland and in South America is told in chapter eleven. While here, however, take time to discover the carvings on top of the flat tabletop-style tombstones which cover their graves. On Don Roberto's stone look for the mark of the brand which he used to identify his cattle when he was a gaucho in Argentina, and on his wife's stone search for the little open-topped thistle. This simple sign represented the couple's strong commitment to the cause of Scottish independence and was probably the first time that this now-accepted Scottish National Party symbol was ever used.

Before walking on into the choir, notice the door on the right through which the dozen or so monks entered after descending the steep, narrow, stone stairs from their dormitory on the first floor to take part in the first service of the morning, and let us follow them through a day in the life of the priory. As befitted their religious calling, the worship of the Augustinian Fathers was never rushed and so it is good to note the stone sedilia, the slightly sloping stone seats. Here the brothers who were not officiating at the altar could seek some rest during the lengthy service.

Search for the piscina, the sink in the wall in which the communion vessels were rinsed at the close of worship. It was designed deliberately without a drain so that the dregs of the communion wine seeped away through the stonework of the church and not a single drop of their goodness was ever washed away and lost. After being washed, the communion cups were carefully stored in the wall aumbry, the little cupboard which can also still be found.

When at last the service was finally over at about 5.00 a.m., the monks left the church in solemn procession through the same door through which they entered, but this time instead of using the stairs, they continued on through the covered cloisters and turned left into the chapter house, which is the best preserved of the priory's buildings. Here the prior sat at the far end, while the other monks sat on the stone seat, which runs round the room. The chapter house takes its name from the fact that it was here each morning that either a chapter from the Bible, or a chapter from the Rules of St Augustine, was read by the prior to the brothers.

Mention of the Rules of St Augustine is a reminder that it was at this early morning hour that the prior was called upon to enforce the discipline of the monastery. Any monk who had perhaps slept in and been late for worship or who had talked during the service or committed some other minor offence, might be sentenced to perform a penance by reciting extra prayers or doing additional work. For more serious offences, however, there was more severe punishment. St Augustine decreed corporal chastisement and the guilty brother was ordered to step forward in the chapter house and prostrate himself so that the prior might punish him with a scourging with his holy rod of correction.

Once the administering of discipline was finished, the prior then moved on to the work of the monastery and issued each of the brothers with their tasks for the day. It was traditionally divided into three parts. The first was devoted to

The church of the Priory of Inchmahome, looking in through the arched west door down the nave to the window in the apse. Being situated out on an island in the centre of the Lake of Menteith has meant that these splendid medieval buildings have survived better than similar buildings on the mainland. (Arthur Down)

prayer and silent meditation in the church and the adjacent covered cloisters; the second part was filled with hard manual tasks preparing food or washing up in the kitchen, cleaning the other rooms in the buildings or digging the priory garden; the remaining third of the monks' waking hours was supposed to be committed to the painstaking mental work of inscribing, illustrating and writing books in the scriptorium or to reading them in the monastery library.

Nowadays the chapter house is used to keep several carved stone effigies under cover and preserved from the elements. They include one of a member of the Augustinian order of monks, who is depicted in his flowing habit, complete with his tonsured 'Polo Mint' hairstyle. There is also a carving of a knight. Most impressive of the carvings is, however, the double effigy of the Countess of Menteith lying side by side in a very loving embrace with her husband, Walter Stewart, who was the Earl of Menteith through his marriage. The sword slanting across his body is said to indicate that he had gone on what was known as a 'caravan', that is he had participated in a crusade, a Holy War of the Cross fought in the Holy Land in Palestine against the Moslem Saracen Turks. Back home safely in Scotland, however, Menteith obviously had time for more leisurely pursuits as carved at his feet is his faithful hunting hound, while at his wife's feet lies her little pet dog. Also on the island is the tomb of their son-in-law, Sir John Drummond, the eighth Thane of Lennox, who was married to their daughter, Lady Christian Stewart, from whose marriage the Earls of Perth and the Viscounts of Strathallan were descended.

Amongst other items of interest collected and displayed in the chapter house are a large flat stone carved with a never-ending Celtic eternity chain and a little simple stone lamp. This was called a crusie or cruesie, a word probably derived from the same word as the crucible used during the mass. It was a simple light, which worked simply by lighting a rush wick floating on a small pool of oil.

At the close of the morning meeting in the chapter house, the prior and the brothers then moved next door into the parlour, whose name was derived from the French verb, *parler*, meaning to speak, as this was the only room in the monastery where they were allowed to talk for a short time about matters other than those of a religious nature. From the little parlour the brothers then moved on to the warming room, again a place where they were allowed a modicum of comfort from the heat of the open fire, whose hearth can still be seen. On the outer wall on the left notice also the little water basin, where the monks washed their hands before entering the frater or refectory to sit down to breakfast, as they were the earliest people to recognise the importance of hygiene and that cleanliness was indeed next to Godliness. Beyond the gable wall of the warming room the remains of the reredorter, the monks' lavatories, can also still be found. Again they were ahead of their times by siting their latrines so that the water of the loch flushed them.

Once seated in the long dining room the brothers were not free simply to relax and enjoy the opportunity to break their fast at last, as while they ate they were expected to listen to the words of the Bible read by one of their fellows standing at a pulpit built into the outer wall. Most of the food which the brothers ate was produced on the island in their own garden, with oats being rowed across to the mainland to be ground into meal for the morning porridge, and the lake itself provided good plump trout as a special treat for feast days. The brothers on Inchmahome are said also to have added to their diet of fish by catching pike in a very unusual fashion. Tradition has it that they tied a perch to the leg of a swan. When a pike took the bait of the perch, the swan created a tremendous commotion and the monks rode out and caught the big pike.

At Inchmahome buildings completely surrounded the cloisters, but sadly they are now reduced to their foundations and so we must surmise where the library and scriptorium to which the monks went on to work were situated. The prior alone had his own private accommodation, which is thought to have been on the first floor of the east range of buildings, and there was also a guest house. This was a most important provision in the days when inns were few and far between and even though Inchmahome was out on an island, it probably received a fair number of travellers seeking food and lodging for the night.

Most important of the visits which the Priory of Inchmahome received, however, were the royal ones. It was visited by three of Scotland's monarchs and these royal visits give some appreciation of the important part which this religious settlement played in the life of Scotland. King Robert the Bruce, of Bannockburn victory fame, came to the island on three occasions in 1306, 1308 and 1310. Some versions of the story of Bannockburn claim that he made a further visit to the island in the form of a pilgrimage to this holy spot, shortly before the impending battle, when he prayed for God's blessing.

Later King Robert II travelled to the priory in 1358, but it was Inchmahome's final royal visit in 1547 which guaranteed the island its lasting place in Scottish history.

Shortly after the Scottish defeat by the English at the Battle of Pinkie near Musselburgh, during England's famous rough wooing of Mary Queen of Scots in an attempt to marry her off to their Prince Edward and thus achieve a binding bond between the two countries, it was decided that not even seemingly impregnable Stirling Castle was strong enough to keep the infant monarch safe from this undesired fate. In September of that year it was therefore decided by the Queen Mother, Mary of Guise and her Scottish advisors that Mary should be brought in secret to Inchmahome, to await the arrival of a French ship to transport her to the French royal court.

Thus it was that the prior and monks of Inchmahome suddenly found themselves host to four-year-old Queen Mary and several of her little companions. What these dedicated, committed bachelors thought about being entrusted with the safety of their little infant queen is not recorded, although there are several traditional stories about how they tried to keep Mary amused, including one about her playing in the monastery garden and another about how the brothers encouraged her to plant a tree. Four hundred years later a boxwood tree in what is known as Queen Mary's Bower is still sometimes pointed out as the one the ill-fated Queen of Scotland planted during her childhood stay, though forestry experts state that it is definitely no more than a hundred years old.

It is interesting to wonder whether the monks on Inchmahome ever heard the words 'Mary, Mary quite contrary, how does your garden grow'. Nowadays it is thought of as simply a children's nursery rhyme, but in Mary's time the words were a vicious satirical attack on the young monarch by the growing number of Scots who were disillusioned by the way in which the Catholic Church was conducting its affairs, their protests leading in 1560 to the Reformation. In the poem the following lines, 'With silver bells and cockle shells and pretty maids all in a row,' referred to the ringing of the bells to indicate the presence of the Host during the Mass, and the superstitious carrying of scallop shells in the hope of warding off seasickness by pilgrims sailing to the holy shrines on the Continent; while, of course, the 'pretty maids' were the young Scottish girls from distinguished families such as the Beatons, Livingstons and Setons who accompanied Mary as her ladies-in-waiting during her stay on Inchmahome and throughout the remainder of her short and tragic reign.

Whether or not the little queen ever did any gardening or planted any tree on Inchmahome, it does seem probable that Mary would have attended some of the services in the priory church, the last time she would worship in Scotland while it was still a Roman Catholic country, and so would certainly have heard the chime of the little silver bells.

In all Mary stayed with her mother, her guardian John, the fifth Lord Erskine, Alexander, the fifth Lord Livingston, her young ladies-in-waiting and her servants on Inchmahome for just under four weeks. Erskine in particular must have appreciated how dangerous the situation was, as his son Robert had been killed by the English at Pinkie. At last, towards the end of their fourth week on the island, the news reached Inchmahome that the French ship under the command of one of the knights of the Order of St John of Jerusalem had at last arrived at Dumbarton on the Clyde to carry Mary and her royal retinue away to France. Sadly she was never to return to Scotland until she was grown up, married and widowed.

After the Reformation, Inchmahome was given as a secular grant to the Erskine family who became its commendators. In the late seventeenth century it became the property of the Dukes of Montrose, who in 1926 handed it over to the care of the Crown. It is now administered by Historic Scotland.

Today Inchmahome is a peaceful rural retreat with pleasant walks around its water lily-edged shores. It is a truly magical place to steal away and enjoy a picnic on a summer day and there are several sheltered spots by the waters of the lake to enjoy such a delight. It seems an unwarranted intrusion, but it is only fair to mention that adjacent to the ferry pier the island is now provided with a small visitor centre with a display about the priory and a shop, operated by Historic Scotland, selling a limited range of guidebooks, confectionery and souvenirs. Nearby there are toilets, but they are not dependent on the waters of the lake to flush them, as were those of the monks in past centuries.

chapter ten

The Lands of
the Moss Lairds

As well as the Lake of Menteith being given Site of Special Scientific Interest status, the adjoining nature reserve to the south and east at Flanders Moss has been similarly classified. This place name, borrowed from the Low Countries, as the Netherlands always used to be referred to in Scotland, well sums up the total pancake-like flatness of this part of Scotland, which does bear comparison with some of the polder lands of Holland.

Once down in the midst of the marsh it is hard to find any distinguishing features. The only landmarks are the distant ones of the Menteith Hills rising to the north and the Campsie Hills which mark the southern boundary of this vast sweep of no-man's-land. It is indeed interesting to find that the few people who live in this hostile environment, perhaps seeking desperately for any kind of territorial identity, still refer to the Menteith Hills as being on the Perthshire side of the river Forth and the Campsies as being on the Stirlingshire side of the river. This is despite the fact that for twenty years following the 1975 Wheatley reform of Scottish local government the whole area was officially in the unimaginatively named Central Region and that since the abolition of this unloved bureaucratic giant in 1995 the entire moss land is now under the control of the even more horribly entitled Stirling Unitary Council.

In earlier centuries similar treacherous marshlands occupied much of the Carse of Stirling. Carse is sometimes also spelt Kerse, but the former spelling, with its anatomical equivalent without the 'c', does seem to suitably emphasise the low-lying nature of the terrain.

This was truly bog land and it is said that knowledge of the few safe causeways across this treacherous territory was often used to great advantage by Rob Roy MacGregor and his compatriots when they came down from the north on their notorious cattle-rustling raids. For the pursuing government dragoons, without local knowledge of the few safe causeways, this featureless countryside must have been a nightmare as they blundered about in search of their evasive quarry.

In the time of Sir William Wallace, in earlier centuries, it was also the existence of this quagmire to the west of Stirling which dictated the siting of the Battle of Stirling Bridge in 1297. Any further downstream would have demanded a fleet of barges to have transported the troops across the Forth, while any further west would have involved countryside impossible for regiments to march across.

As well as influencing history, the moss lands also obviously have a marked effect on the whole geography of this area on the edge of the Trossachs as they make the progress of both the river Forth and its major tributary the Teith decidedly slow and sluggish. After passing under the bridge beside the Trossachs Inn, which carries the A81 from Glasgow to Aberfoyle, the Forth enters upon its most uninteresting stretch as it becomes bogged down in navigating Gartrenich Moss. The monotony of this section of the river is relieved only by the fact that it is along it that it is joined by its first major feeder stream, the Keltie Burn, and that near their confluence is a long row of old cottages, now converted into an attractive single house with the intriguing name of Barbados.

From there the Forth proceeds on at the same unhurried pace for a further 6 miles, until it finally escapes from the peat lands and at last emerges into some fertile farm fields. Between Cardross House and Parks of Garden, it flows under the old stone bridge which carries the B8034 to Port of Menteith. The historic bridge was erected in 1774, paid for with funds confiscated from the Jacobite lairds after the failure of the 1745 rebellion. Its three arches carry the road over a distance of 200ft, which shows how the Forth is at this point in its course beginning to broaden in width.

Continuing downstream the Forth then passes South Flanders Farm before its north bank becomes the boundary of the even more descriptively named Faraway Farm. Faraway really is, as its name states, 'faraway'! To reach this isolated spot it is necessary to first drive past two other farms and then on again over a narrow box girder bridge before finally coming to this lonely farmhouse in the middle of nowhere. Once there at Faraway Farm it is very puzzling to imagine why it was ever built where it stands, the explanation being that originally the farm consisted of only the 12 arable acres nearest to it, and that it was not until much later that the eventual clearance of the moss enabled it to expand to the much larger 200 acres which it now covers. Such a dramatic expansion all came about because of the pioneering work of one landowner, the celebrated Scottish law lord, Lord Kames.

In 1766 Lord Kames bought the neighbouring estate of Blair Drummond, which is now well known as the site of Scotland's only safari park, whose African lions, elephants and hundreds of other tropical animals now roam its still flat, but now dry, landscape. Back in the eighteenth century when Kames made his purchase, he knew full well that 1,800 of Blair Drummond's 2,000 acres was covered with a 12ft-deep layer of the accursed peat moss, but hoped that his previous experience of land reclamation would enable him to get rid of this blanket and turn the ground beneath into good farming land, thus greatly enhancing the value of his new acquisition. The problem was how to reach this rich alluvial soil which he was certain lay underneath, because several previous attempts to do so by digging had failed, defeated by the sheer enormity of the task.

Lord Kames decided that he must think up a much faster method of removing the moss and concluded that the secret was to employ water power. He therefore employed a large squad of labourers to start digging canals along which to float the moss to the nearby river Forth. The idea worked, but the cost of the labourers' wages made it uneconomical, and, when it seemed that the scheme would have to be abandoned, the wily law lord came up with a way of getting the work done for nothing. From his knowledge of Scottish current affairs Kames knew that the terrible clearances instituted by his fellow landowners in the Highlands, who wanted to make more money by clearing their estates to graze sheep, were resulting in many crofters being forced to emigrate to Canada, New Zealand and other colonies. He reckoned that if he could offer the labourers plots of land on his estate in return for clearing the moss, many would prefer to move south to Blair Drummond rather than have to make the much more dangerous journey overseas and that the rugged crofters used to working outdoors all year round in all types of weather would be the ideal men to do the back-breaking work.

Kames therefore advertised that he would provide each Highland family which took up his offer with a 10-acre lowland croft with guaranteed tenure and a promise of freedom from rent for the first seven years. As a further bait for the shrewd Highlanders, he also promised that until they were able to grow their own food on their 10 acres, he would provide enough meal for them to make porridge for their whole family; and went on to remind them that the abundance of peat right on their doorsteps would guarantee them warmth while they did the task.

In 1769 the first of the crofters arrived at Blair Drummond, much to the terror of the existing local inhabitants who had heard bloodcurdling rumours about these wild Highlanders. It was definitely a case of lock up your daughters and your valuables as the crofting families moved in because it was alleged that they were often very violent, especially when under the influence of alcohol, which was the case most of the time. Very soon they sarcastically dubbed the newcomers the Moss Lairds and became even more suspicious of them when they discovered that they spoke no English, but only Gaelic. To make matters still worse, stories spread that the crofters were not even building houses for themselves, but were making their homes in holes in the moss. This was indeed true, but far from proving how primitive the crofters were, it was a sign of their true Highland guile. For they had quickly discovered that as little as a footstep vibrated anything up to 50 yards and that stone- or brick-built houses would have collapsed quite easily, as if hit by an earthquake. On the other hand, by digging down into the moss and thatching the top with heather, they found they could make safe temporary dwelling places.

How the Highland crofters achieved this was described by Bo'ness colliery owner and well-known Victorian geologist Henry M. Cadell in his book

The Story of the Forth. First, the Moss Laird, helped by his wife and children, together dug a deep trench down to the bottom of the moss and right round the site which they had chosen for their home. From the centre of this square ditch they then scooped out the remaining peat, 'as a child hollows out the heart of a turnip to make a lantern at Halloween', as Cadell vividly describes it. The walls of the resultant peat homes were as high as 12ft to begin with, but as the moisture in the moss evaporated into the surrounding air, they quickly shrank until they were less than half that height but still about a yard wide, thus maintaining their insulation. They were then roofed with the timber which Lord Kames provided free of charge and, once thatched with the heather which grew in abundance all around them, it was difficult to identify them from the surrounding countryside. While their lowland neighbours condemned these peat houses as unfit for human habitation and fit only for animals, the Highlanders who lived in them were well pleased with their snug wee homes, which being so low lying were also well protected from the westerly wind which often whipped across the expanse of moss lands.

Gradually however, as they won their battle with the moss, the Highlanders began to build more conventional farmhouses for themselves and, through their hard work and law-abiding natures, convinced their neighbours that they had nothing to fear. Lord Kames, who was over seventy when he began his ambitious clearance scheme at Blair Drummond, died in 1782, when the job was still unfinished, but his son George Hume continued the project and further encouraged the strong Protestant work ethic of his Highland workforce by providing prizes of ploughs and bags of seed for those who cleared the most land in the shortest time.

Most importantly, Hume made the work of the Moss Lairds easier by investing in the construction of a large wooden waterwheel, which he had erected where the river Teith flows into the Forth. It is interesting to note that at the confluence of the two rivers, the Teith carries the greater flow of water and the greatly increased water power which it provided made it easier for the Highlanders to float away the moss. Hume also brought the Moss Lairds more into touch with their neighbours by building stone roads, thus linking their homes with the road from Aberfoyle to the village of Thornhill.

His enterprise was noted by several of the other landlords in the area, who subsequently copied his example and employed crofters from the Highlands on their estates, so that by 1811 there were around 150 Moss Lairds and their families, totalling almost 1,000 people, involved in the task of clearing ever-increasing stretches of Blair Drummond moss, Cardross moss, Kincardine-in-Menteith moss and Flanders moss.

Hume also helped to have the road to Stirling greatly improved and this encouraged the Moss Lairds to add to their income by digging the peat and selling it to the townsfolk as fuel for their fires. As their fortunes improved, the Moss Lairds decided that their bairns must be educated, and, again helped by George Hume who paid part of the dominie's salary, a school was established. Over the years the Moss Lairds continued to prosper and were able to buy live-

The lofty spire of the strange school building erected to educate the children of the Moss Lairds can be seen for miles across the flat farmlands of the Carse of Stirling. The school has been closed for many years and is now an unusual private house, which most recently came on the market in March 1999. (William F. Hendrie)

stock at the local market in Stirling and lay the foundations for the prosperous farms seen nowadays around Thornhill, where, far from it being considered a stigma to be known to be descended from the original Moss Lairds, it is now a mark of honour.

Thornhill itself is an immaculately neat and tidy little place with rows of old low-roofed cottages and two-storey houses lining both sides of the long main street. Many of the buildings are attractively colour-washed, adding an almost continental touch to this douce Scottish village. Along the length of the main street, tourist buses and cars race, intent on reaching the lochs and mountains as quickly as possible, but it is well worth stopping in Thornhill because this eastern entrance to the Trossachs possesses two excellent traditional Scottish pubs. At one end of the street stands The Crown and at the other end is situated The Lion and the Unicorn, whose colourful frontage boasts one of the most beautifully painted inn signs in Scotland. On a journey to or from the Trossachs,

both are good places to stop to enjoy a bite to eat, as they both provide good traditional Scottish food, from home-made soup to steak pies.

At one end the entrance to Thornhill is guarded by the turreted premises of the local Masonic Lodge and at the other by the towering spire of Norrieston parish church. Today Norrieston is linked with the parish kirk at Kincardine-in-Menteith, which means the two churches share a minister, based in Thornhill, but still keep their independence by having their own sessions and boards. The name Norrieston comes from the hamlet or little township of farm cottages and other buildings which grew up around the farm founded by Gabriel Norrie.

Two other farm names in the Thornhill area with a story attached to them are Spittal and Upper Spittal. They were founded by a man named Robert, who back in the early 1500s was the tailor to King James IV, nicknamed 'Scotland's Most Curious King' because of his quest to lead the world in the discovery, amongst many other things, of how to convert base metal into gold and how to fly. He appears also to have had expensive tastes for the latest fashions, because, as the royal tailor, Robert made a small fortune. He used his money to found a hospital near the castle in Stirling and thus became known as Robert Spittal. The name stuck and so, when he came to live at Coldoch, about 3 miles from Thornhill, the farms he established on his lands also became known as Spittal and Upper Spittal.

Near Ruskie is little Loch Ruskie, from which the hamlet of cottages and impressive-looking, solid stone-built Ruskie Hall take their name. In the middle of the loch is an island and on it the ruins of the castle which was the home of Sir John Menteith, who has the unenviable claim to fame of being the Scot who

Above Well-tended floral hanging baskets, flower-packed window boxes and colour washes on the façades of its houses and cottages help greatly to brighten Thornhill's long Main Street. (Arthur Down)

Opposite The Crown Hotel on Thornhill's Main Street. (William F. Hendrie)

betrayed Sir William Wallace to the English. He is believed to be buried on Inchmahome, but no grave on the island bears his name.

Another view of Thornhill Main Street.

Near Ruskie is an attraction for those who enjoy gardening, Blairhoyle Nursery. It is open from March to October, but only during afternoons and not on Tuesdays. Blairhoyle specialises in Scottish heathers, including white heather which is considered lucky, alpine plants, conifers and shrubs. Tucked away behind a long estate wall, the nursery is a peaceful relaxing place to enjoy a leisurely browse through an interesting collection of flowers and trees and, once inside the gate, there is ample parking space.

From Blairhoyle along the A873 it is a short drive west to the junction of the A81, which continues straight ahead to Port of Menteith and Aberfoyle, before turning south to Glasgow. Turning north at the road junction before the Lake of Menteith takes drivers back to Callander.

Chapter Eleven

Don Roberto, Scotland's Gaucho

Like Thornhill and Ruskie, another village on the edge of the Trossachs which rarely attracts visitors is Gartmore, a short distance to the south of Aberfoyle. Although many tourists speed by it on the A81 road from Glasgow to the Trossachs, few turn off to explore quiet little Gartmore. This is a pity because by missing it out of their itineraries, they miss seeing the large monument to one of Scotland's most interesting characters, Don Roberto. Now largely forgotten, Don Roberto, despite his foreign-sounding title, was in his day one of the most famous men in Scotland.

Tall, red-haired and romantically handsome, Don Roberto was born Robert Bontine Cunninghame Graham, the oldest son of Graham of Gartmore, in London in 1852. He was brought up at Gartmore House, a seventeenth-century, three-storey, whitewashed mansion, which still stands behind his monument on the far side of the village playing field. By day young Robert loved to roam the Trossachs on his pony, which was one of many horses kept in Gartmore House's stables, while by night he revelled in the stories of riding and adventure in South America, which his beautiful young mother, who was of Spanish descent, told him by the inglenook fire. Robert's father, who was a soldier, was often ill as a result of a wound which he received during a riot in Ireland.

At the age of thirteen, Robert was sent south to England to complete his education at Harrow School in London. After the freedom of life in the Trossachs he did not take kindly to the many rules and regulations of his public school and was punished by beatings with the cane and the birch rod on several occasions. He did, however, prove to be a good pupil, especially at foreign languages which he appeared to master with ease. He was also good at sports, especially fencing at which he represented the school.

His schooldays over, in 1869 Robert returned to Scotland and learned for the first time that the Graham family finances were in such a poor state that his beloved Gartmore House would have to be let. Disappointed at being deprived of the opportunity to develop the Gartmore Estate, Robert instead decided to go abroad to seek the fortune needed to bring Gartmore back under his control. Inspired no doubt by his mother's childhood tales, he travelled to South America, but found it riven with civil war and disease. He caught typhus and was forced to recuperate in Uruguay. Later he was involved in the fighting with rebels on both sides of the war. To escape the troubles he moved to Paraguay, where he tried to improve his fortunes by growing green tea, but failed because of lack of funds.

With the last of his money he bought a passage home and in London became the talk of the town when he strode out wearing the poncho cape, flowing trousers and wide-brimmed sombrero hat of a gaucho cowboy. By 1876 he had saved enough to sail back to South America, this time to the Argentine, and he soon got a job driving horses from Uruguay to Brazil to supply that country's cavalry. With his profits he and some friends bought an *estancia*, but before his ranching career could develop it was attacked and wrecked by bandits.

Once again Roberto, as he had by then become known, returned home. His next journey was to France in 1878, and it was in Paris that he found himself captivated by a stunningly beautiful young lady called Gabrielle de la Baltmondiere, who let it be known that she was an exiled princess from Chile. She was in fact a very good young actress, who had run away from her Yorkshire home where her father was a surgeon.

Whether or not Don Roberto knew the truth about her background before he married his seventeen-year-old bride mattered little, because she made him the ideal wife. Like him she was an expert rider, loved to travel, shared his interests in photography and writing and had similar radical views, campaigning in particular for women's rights. Gallantly Don Roberto never revealed his wife's secret past and she always remained his Chilean princess, with all of the regal manner to go with it. As well as her stunning good looks, she had an equally lively personality which well complemented that of Don Roberto himself.

By this time Don Roberto had saved enough to reclaim Gartmore House from its current tenants and he brought the lovely Gabrielle back to live in Scotland. There she impressed the gardeners on the Gartmore Estate with her knowledge of botany and made a collection of plants, which still exists in the possession of the Smith Museum in Stirling. At the same time she shocked the other members of the Graham family by smoking small cigars, a habit she claimed to have picked up to keep mosquitoes and flies at bay during her travels in South America.

The Cunninghame Grahams were even more shocked when the young couple espoused left-wing politics. In 1886 Don Roberto stood as the radical Liberal candidate for the constituency of North Lanarkshire and was elected Member of Parliament. In his maiden speech he referred to 'the society in which capital and this luxury makes Heaven for 30,000 and a Hell for 30,000,000' and this became his theme throughout his parliamentary career. As it progressed he moved further to the left and became the first chairman of the Independent Scottish Labour Party. Its policies included the nationalisation of land and, of all minerals, the abolition of the House of Lords and home rule, and it was no surprise that he later became first President of the Scottish National Party.

The romantic figure of Don Roberto, Scotland's famous gaucho. Robert Bontine Cunninghame Graham is engraved on his memorial overlooking the village green at Gartmore, where as a boy he used to ride his pony. (Arthur Down)

In the House of Commons Don Roberto's outspoken views often got him into trouble. On one occasion he was advised by the Speaker to withdraw his critical comments. He replied, 'I never withdraw!', a remark copied by the playwright George Bernard Shaw in *Arms and the Man*. Shaw is also said to have been influenced by Don Roberto's adventures when he wrote *Man and Superman* and *Captain Brassbound's Conversion*. When Shaw's mother encountered Don Roberto she asked who he was and, when told that this was Cunninghame Graham, declared: 'Nonsense! Cunninghame Graham is one of your Socialists. That man is a gentleman!'

Gentleman or not, Cunninghame Graham landed himself in prison when he attended a huge rally in Trafalgar Square on 13 November 1887. The rally turned violent as the police battered the crowd and Don Roberto's protests led to his arrest. He was sentenced to six weeks in prison. Later, when he became Deputy Lord Lieutenant of Stirlingshire and a Justice of the Peace, he issued the photograph of himself in prison uniform as his official calling card. Don Roberto must have made an unusual Justice of the Peace as he actively campaigned against most court penalties and fought for prison reform. Remembering the thrashings which he had himself endured as a boy at Harrow he led the campaign against corporal punishment, demanding in the House that birching of juveniles and the flogging of adults with the cat o' nine tails should both be abolished. He fought against sentences involving penalties of hard labour and when two girls received such a sentence in 1888 for sleeping rough in London, he was successful in having it rescinded. Amongst many other causes, he also campaigned against capital punishment and British colonialism, describing Rhodesia as 'Fraudesia' and criticised this country's involvement in the Boer War in South Africa.

At the same time, however, Don Roberto and Gabrielle had no hesitation in developing their own ranching interests in South America. They also travelled in Mexico and the United States, where, during a visit to Texas, Don Roberto was thrilled to meet up with Colonel Bill Cody, the legendary Buffalo Bill. Other adventures included an expedition to North Africa and a search in Spain for a long-forgotten Roman gold mine.

Unfortunately all of these varied enterprises did not raise enough money for Don Roberto and Gabrielle to continue to maintain Gartmore House, and, after living there for seventeen years, they were eventually forced to sell their handsome mansion and the surrounding estate to a shipping magnate. Worse news was to follow in 1906 when Don Roberto learned that Gabrielle was seriously ill in France. He rushed to be with her and was at her bedside when she died at the age of forty-five. Her body was brought home to Scotland and, with a lone piper playing a lament, was rowed across the Lake of Menteith to be buried in the chancel of the Augustinian priory on the island of Inchmahome, which was the Graham family's traditional burial place. Helped by only the oldest of his family servants, Don Roberto personally dug the grave in the ruins of the old priory, where his much-adored Gabrielle was laid to rest.

Despite his grief, Don Roberto lived for many years after Gabrielle's death. At the start of the First World War in 1914, despite his strong anti-war philosophy, he volunteered to serve his country by joining the army, despite the fact that he was by then sixty-two. He was appointed lieutenant-colonel and was sent to South America to buy horses. It was a task which he loved. 'God forbid that I should go to any heaven in which there are no horses,' he once wrote when he sent a donation to American President Theodore Roosevelt to help erect an equestrian statue to the memory of Colonel Bill Cody.

Once peace returned, Don Roberto continued his interest in politics, although he had long before lost his Parliamentary seat, and throughout the 1920s he championed the cause of Scottish Nationalism. In 1936 he sailed back to South America where, shortly afterwards, he died in Argentina at the age of eighty-three. He was as famous there as he was in Scotland and his funeral service in the capital Buenos Aires was attended by the country's president and all of its political leaders. His hearse was pulled by two of his favourite horses, both wearing black plumes and led by two of the gauchos from his ranch. After the service his body was put aboard a ship and brought back home to Scotland, where, like his wife, he had given orders that he was to be buried on Inchmahome. At the funeral ceremony, strands of hair from his three favourite horses were laid on the coffin and the flat tombstone which covers his grave was engraved with the distinctive mark with which he had always branded his cattle on the Argentinian *estancia*.

A full-life portrait of Don Roberto, with his bushy, curly hair and neatly shaped, pointed beard, painted by Sir John Lavery, hangs in the art gallery at Glasgow's Kelvingrove Museum, while his beautifully tooled South American-style leather saddle, long stock whip and lasso are in the safekeeping of the Smith Gallery in Stirling, but the largest memorial to him is appropriately in Gartmore within sight of the house where he grew up.

For such a true Scot, it is appropriate that the monument on the edge of the village green is looked after by the National Trust for Scotland. The memorial contains stones donated by the governments of Argentina and Uruguay and it was unveiled on this site on 1981 after being moved from Dumbarton Rock overlooking the river Clyde, where it was originally erected in 1936. Buried below the stones of the monument is one of the hooves of Pampa, one of Don Roberto's best-loved horses in Scotland, which he rescued from life as a cab horse and to whom he dedicated one of his thirty books. An inscription reads, 'To Pampa, my black Argentine, who I rode for twenty years without a fall. May the earth lie on him as lightly as he once trod upon its face. Vale... or until so long. Don Roberto.'

The monument also incorporates a commemorative stone to another of his favourite mounts, Pingo. It originally stood at Gartahan Home Farm, where Pingo died. Although his monument, as Don Roberto would have wished, concentrates much on his horses, the man himself is not forgotten and the inscription sums him up by stating, 'Robert Bontine Cunninghame Graham, 1852-1936. He was a master of life and a king among men. Farmer, author, traveller and horseman, patriot Scot and citizen of the world as betokened by the stones above. Died in Argentine, interred on Inchmahome.'

After Don Roberto and Gabrielle were forced by financial circumstances to part with Gartmore House, it became the home of the well-known Cayzer family of shipping line fame. They looked after it well and during the summer season it was often the scene of parties and gatherings of their friends. Several members of the Cayzer family lie buried at Gartmore parish church. The family name is also still remembered in Gartmore through the local place name Cayzer Court.

Later, Gartmore was acquired by the Roman Catholic Church who converted it into an approved school for delinquent teenage boys, who were cared for and taught by priests. When residential treatment of young offenders went out of fashion, to be replaced by the non-punitive approach of the Scottish children's panels with their policy of trying to cope by caring for delinquents in their own communities, Gartmore was acquired by an American fundamentalist religious group called The Way. After many years of tough usage as an approved school, Gartmore required a great deal of work to be done on it and its new American owners spared no expense in repairing it and returning it to something approaching its former glory. They also proved good neighbours by contributing funds to the village Church of Scotland parish kirk.

Gartmore Church was originally built in 1790 and was modernised and improved in 1872. With a congregation of around one hundred, Gartmore is linked with neighbouring Bucklyvie and both churches are served by one minister.

In addition to its kirk, Gartmore has a lively community life, the highlight of which each year is its annual gala day. It includes a procession around the village streets, a fancy dress competition and sports on the playing field.

Gartmore House is now a Christian holiday retreat and conference centre. Its premises offer excellent modern facilities to its guests but, apart from catering for its residents, it is not open to visitors. The well-known old Black Bull Hotel in the Main Street does, however, make visitors warmly welcome. It is a comfortable spot to enjoy a bar meal and a drink before leaving peaceful little Gartmore to return to the busier, better known parts of the Trossachs.

Callander town walk

Start at the car park on the site of the town's former railway station in Station Road, reached by turning right at the north end of Main Street. Toilets are available.

As you leave the car park, notice on the left the old iron railway bridge which carries the road over the tracks which formerly carried the trains operated by the Caledonian Railway Co. south to Stirling. Twenty yards further on the right the former tracks have been converted into a walking and cycling path which runs 9½ miles through wooded countryside to the village of Strathyre.

Look up at the turreted façade of the early nineteenth-century stone-built, slate-roofed, turreted Dreadnought Hotel, originally opened in 1802, which derives its name from the war cry of the Clan McNab.

Walk on past the two silver-painted stone lions which guard the porticoed front entrance to the Dreadnought Hotel.

On the opposite side of Station Road, to the left notice the post office with its postbox at the entrance dating from the reign of King George V.

At the west end of Station Road cross Main Street at the lights-controlled pedestrian crossing.

This is a good point to note the original layout of the town, as it was developed as a planned settlement following the defeat of the Jacobites in 1746 with broad Main Street running form north to south and transected by three shorter, narrower streets from east to west.

Walk 20 yards north along Leny Road.

Notice on the right the façade of the Dreadnought Hotel, with its painted carving of the McNab chieftain.

Turn left into the lane leading to the car park on the shores of the river Teith.

Notice the magnificent view north to where 2,875ft-high Ben Ledi, the Mountain of the Gods, dominates the scene.

After admiring the view of the river Teith, which is a tributary of the river Forth, climb the steps on the left to the summit of the Hill of St Kessog.

St Kessog is believed to have been a follower of St Columba of Iona and to have brought Christianity to the lands around the shores of Loch Lomond, where a church was dedicated to him in the village of Luss and in the lands to the south of Callander. St Kessog is believed to have preached to his followers from this vantage point in the sixth century and, after he was martyred, it is thought that much later in 1232 a church dedicated to his memory was erected at the foot of this hill, the foundations of which were unearthed in excavations conducted by Cllr John Glen, Provost of Callander, during the 1930s.

Descend the steps.

The shape of the Hill of St Kessog suggests that it may at a later date have been the site of a wooden motte or small castle. If so, its protective bailey would have surrounded the base of the hill and within there would have been simple lean-to buildings for various support trades such as cartwrights and hammersmiths. St Kessog's Fair was held here on 10 March each year until the nineteenth century.

Take the path on the town side of the Hill of St Kessog, whose grassy slopes were used as bow butts to support archery targets in the Middle Ages. At the end of the path turn right into Bridge Street and, after 10 yards, enter the old graveyard through the double wrought-iron gates.

The gravestones date from the eighteenth century and this graveyard is thought to have replaced an older one beside the original church at the foot of the Hill of St Kessog. The unusual hexagonal tower built into the boundary wall on the right is a watchtower erected at the beginning of the nineteenth century to guard bodies in newly dug graves from the threat of being snatched by the resurrectionists, who, during this period, were paid to deliver corpses to the anatomy schools at both Edinburgh and Glasgow Universities to enable the medical students to practise dissection. The names of the local tradesmen, including the joiner and the masons who built the tower, are recorded on the lintel above the entrance door. Notice the mountain ash or rowan tree which bears bright red berries and was believed to scare witches from haunting the graveyard.

Leave the graveyard and turn right, continuing down Bridge Street to the bridge over the river Teith.

The plaque on the stone parapet on the right-hand side of the bridge notes that it was opened in 1908, when Cllr Alex Scott was Provost of Callander and Lt Home Drummond was Convener of Stirlingshire. Notice the two original wrought-iron lamp standards at either end of the stone parapet on the left-hand side of the bridge.

On the west side of the bridge continue to walk along Bridge Street, passing several fine examples of Scottish housing: white-harled Teith View House on the right opposite the three storey Teithside House which stands in its own grounds on the left.

Note the traditional slate roofs of these properties and others in Bridge Street as well as the large number of chimney pots, which are a reminder that their rooms were all heated by open coal fires in the decades before the introduction of gas, oil and electrical central heating.

Walk on past the Tudor-style black and white frontage of the Bridgend House Hotel. Beyond it, Ivy Cottage boasts an unusual stone above the front door, carved with the tools of the masons' trade. Walk on past the low single-storey, white-harled cottages, which date from the late eighteenth or early nineteenth century, and look at the unusually shaped, stone-built, two-storey Ardess House with its slated roof. Cross the entrance to Oakbank Lane.

Note the curved stone at the foot of the wall on the far side which was placed there to safeguard the wall of the building from damage by cart wheels as they turned into this narrow entrance. The building on the far side is now a private residence, but it was originally a chapel and the stone above the front door still bears the inscription from the New Testament, John Chapter 3 verse 16: God so loved the world, that He gave His only begotten son (etc.).

Continue to the far end of Bridge Street where it branches left to Invertrossachs, which is a pleasant walk, and right to the main A81 road to Glasgow which, half a mile further on, passes the modern premises of McLaren High School and the adjacent modern Callander Leisure Centre and swimming pool. Take care crossing this busy main road and start walking back east along the opposite side of Bridge Street, passing more stone-built residential properties. Cross the entrance to Manse Lane, whose name indicates that it was the site of the home of the parish minister. Three-storey traditionally built East Mains House is now a bed and breakfast establishment. Pass Acharn House on your left, noticing the unusual carving of a bearded head above the front door. Continuing on, stop to look at imposing three-storey Robertson House.

The front garden of the house is guarded by wrought-iron gates. Notice, however, the stumps of iron along the length of the garden wall which show where the original iron railings were removed with an acetylene burner in 1942 following a government order that they must be sacrificed to provide metal for the war effort. While this gesture may have boosted civilian morale, it is disappointing to record that the resulting scrap iron was unsuitable and was left in rusting piles until after peace returned in 1945.

Walk on, stopping to admire the fine stone-built premises of Callander primary school with its curved, pillared and porticoed front entrance on the far side of the playground. This was originally the town's secondary school until the building of the new McLaren High School. Turn into School Lane and look up to see the date stone on the east façade of the school building and untangle the figures indicating that it was constructed in 1906. Walk on past the modern premises of Callander nursery school and after 200 yards turn left to re-cross the river Teith by the pedestrian bridge. At the far end on the east side stop to look at the sundial.

Dated 1756, the sundial bears the interesting inscription, 'I mark not the hours unless they are bright, I mark not the hours of darkness and night, My promise is solely to the sun, To point out the course his chariot doth run'. On the ground note the modern addition of a plaque on which is inscribed 'Non rego, Nisi regor', which translated from the Latin reads, 'I don't rule the time unless I'm ruled corrected', which is followed by the information that British Summer Time is Greenwich Mean Time plus sixty minutes.

Before moving on along South Church Street, try one of the unusual seats jutting out from the stone wall surrounding the sundial. Pass the modern premises on the right housing the public library, police station and mountain rescue headquarters.

On the left notice attractive Waterside Cottage and beyond it Airlie Cottage, whose gardens run down to the banks of the river Teith. Next door note white-harled Waterside House.

Walk on and to the right you'll pass the unusually designed stone-built premises of Callander parish church, with its tall clock tower erected in 1907. On the left pass Norwood Bed and Breakfast and Highland House Hotel, which in summer is decorated with colourful flower baskets. Beyond it White Shutters also offers bed and breakfast accommodation. Cross Church Street to look at the Victorian church hall built in 1849 and modernised in 1991. Enter the Millennium Garden in front of the hall to see St Kessog's bell, which rang to summon people to worship from 1784 to 1985. Straight ahead on the opposite side of Main Street, notice imposing stone-built Struan House. At the junction turn right and walk along Main Street past Aros Lane.

Stop to look across Main Street to note the carved juncture stone above the door of the house opposite which records the initials of the husband and wife who originally built and occupied it.

After 400 yards further on turn right into the long driveway which leads to Roman Camp Hotel.

The buildings date from 1625 and the name is derived from a belief that a Roman legion camped near where it is situated.

After admiring the façade of the hotel, exit by the lane to the south and on reaching Main Street cross to the opposite east side. Walk back towards the centre of Callander.

Allow time to visit Hamilton Toy Museum, whose five display rooms are crowded with delightful memories of childhood. Further towards the town centre the Kings' new and second-hand bookshop is also well worth a stop to browse through its contents and make a purchase or two.

After leaving the bookshop cross the entrance to North Church Street and continue along Main Street past the Highland Art Studios on the corner.

On the left-hand side of Main Street notice the three-storey premises of the Waverley Hotel, named after the hero of Sir Walter Scott's Waverley novels. On the right the Ben Ledi Ice Cream Parlour and Fish and Chip Shop is famed for its delicious treats.

At Ancaster Square cross Main Street to examine the tall stone column of the town war memorial, which is dominated by Scotland's national heraldic beast the Lion Rampant.

On the south side of Ancaster Square, Campbell the Butcher sells traditional Scottish products including haggis, black and white puddings and square slicing Lorne sausage; all worth sampling.

Re-cross Main Street to admire the impressive façade of St Kessog's kirk with its tall clock tower and spire.

The premises have been converted into the Rob Roy Visitor Centre, which houses an audio-visual show telling the story of the famous Scottish outlaw. The ground floor also accommodates the local information and tourist office.

On leaving the Rob Roy Centre walk to the right around the building and on the right you will see the former stone-built nineteenth-century church hall with its attractive entrance porch which now leads into a café. Beyond the hall walk past the car park of St Joseph's Roman Catholic Church, which is used on Saturdays for car boot sales, to see the front façade of the church which is decorated with a plaster relief depicting Joseph and Mary with the infant Jesus on horseback. Return along Glenartley Court to your left.

On the right, behind the former St Kessog's kirk, note the monument erected in July 1899 to the memory of Callander's former town clerk, lawyer (the Scottish name for a solicitor) and banker William C. McMichael, who was 'A wise counsellor and a true friend'.

Walk to the right round the church back into Ancaster Square and, after looking at the modern fountains which spout from the stone terrace to the left, exit the square back into Main Street, passing the premises of Callander's famous fudge and tablet makers, Johnsons. Continue walking north and note the impressive stone-built premises of the Bank of Scotland on the opposite side of the street to your right and the Royal Bank of Scotland to the left. The large four-storey stone-built premises of the former Drummond Arms hotel, now converted into shops and business premises, are passed on the left before crossing the entrance to Cross Street. One hundred yards further on pass the entrance to Bridge Street to the right and continue along Main Street passing the traditional mortar and pestle sign outside the chemist shop on the left. Pass the Crown, which is one of the town's oldest pubs. A few yards further on the left a former bank office has been converted into a restaurant, with an imposing entrance vestibule. After passing it walk on north before turning to the right into Station Road and returning to the car park.

Aberfoyle village walk

Start at the car park in the centre of the village beside the Trossachs
Discovery Information Centre, where toilets are available.

After visiting the centre, watching the audio-visual show and inspecting the 3D map of the area, turn right as you leave and walk through the car park past the garden centre on the right to Manse Road. The name Manse Road is a reminder that the parish minister's house was originally in this street.

Look to the right and you will see the three-storey premises of the former Bailie Nicol Jarvie Hotel, which, along with its stables and coach houses, is being redeveloped as residential housing. The hotel took its name from a character in Sir Walter Scott's novel, *Rob Roy*.

In the grounds of the former hotel garden in front of you still stands the Poker Tree, an ancient oak on whose trunk a red-painted poker was traditionally attached to represent the improvised weapon, pulled red hot from the fire, which the redoubtable Bailie wielded in what is described in Scott's novel as 'the affray at the Clachan of Aberfoyle'.

Turn left into Manse Road and cross the narrow stone-built humpbacked Forth
Bridge.

The bridge was erected in 1715 and replaced an earlier wooden structure. It was near here that Highland cattle drovers formerly forded the shallow waters with their cows. Take in the view to the right of 3,192ft-high Ben Lomond.

Walk 200 yards past modern sheltered homes to the site of the original
clachan, or hamlet, of Aberfoyle. Enter the churchyard through the gate on the
left. Walk on through the graveyard to the ruins of the original parish church
whose entrance is flanked on either side by two heavy metal mort safes.

During the early decades of the nineteenth century mort safes were placed over newly dug graves to protect bodies from being snatched by the dreaded resurrectionists, who were paid to supply fresh specimens to the schools of anatomy at both the universities of Edinburgh and Glasgow to enable medical students to practise dissection. Why the Kirk Session at Aberfoyle felt it necessary to invest in the purchase of two expensive mort safes for their small community is not clear. Aberfoyle has always been a place of many mysteries.

Enter the church to find the gravestone of the Revd Robert Kirk, the parish minister alleged to have been spirited away by the fairies. After leaving the church and graveyard take the path to the left which leads, after about 400 yards, to the foot of Doon Hill around which there is a circular track.

Doon is the Gaelic word for fairy, and it was on the slopes of this hill that the village minister believed that he met the fairies, elves and other little people about whom he wrote.

Climb the steep path to the summit of Doon Hill, where the tallest tree is still known as the Minister's Pine. Descend from the hill and return to Manse Road. Turn right and, walking back to the Forth Bridge, notice the flat flood plain of the river to which modern prevention methods offer protection.

Ponies often graze in the fields on either side of the road and are a reminder that the outdoor pastime of pony trekking had its origins in Aberfoyle during the years following the Second World War.

On the left pass the entrance to the narrow road which leads to the Covenanters Inn.

The inn was one of the original pony-trekking bases and is still a popular local hostelry. Its whitewashed walls and connections with horse riding led, in the 1950s and 1960s, to the nickname Ponderosa.

Re-cross the Forth Bridge and walk to the junction of Manse Road and Loch Ard Road.

Loch Ard Road leads past the stone-built village primary school and Victorian parish church on the right to Milton, Kinlochard and on 12 miles to Stronachlachar and a further 3 miles to Inversnaid on the shores of Loch Lomond, where Rob Roy's Cave is situated.

Turn right and walk the 20 yards to where Loch Ard Road joins Main Street.

On the left is the start of the Duke's Pass, the steep, winding hill road which leads to Aberfoyle Community Centre and to the Forest Park Visitor Centre.

Walk past the post office at which a post bus is based to carry both mail and passengers to surrounding rural addresses.

On the left notice the Clachan Bar, which first opened in 1885, and on the right the more modern Forth Inn, part of the Pavilion building erected in the early 1960s.

Continue past the curio shop on the left. It was originally the village grocer and its wooden fitments still surround its interior. Pass the police station on the left and climb the stone steps to the terrace in front of Viewforth Terrace.

Note the red sandstone with which it and the neighbouring Tudor 'magpie'-style block were constructed after it was brought to the village as ballast on the first goods train to travel to the village.

At the far end of the terrace, turn left and walk up the slope to visit the Green Art Gallery. On leaving, pass the historic nineteenth-century white-harled premises which now house the headquarters of the Trossachs Cab Co. and on the left notice the Old Coach House, now converted into a restaurant and bar. Continue walking east, passing on the right the award-winning traditional Scottish butchers' whose meat and home-made haggis and sausages are worth sampling. Next door The Red Herring, supplier of that other staple of Scottish diet, fish and chips, is sadly currently closed. On the left pass St Mary's Episcopalian Church on the hillside and notice its unusual weather-vane in the shape of the early Christian symbol of a fish.

High above the church rise the slopes of Limecraig, which takes its name from the lime kilns formerly worked there. The lower slopes of Limecraig are the site of Dounans Residential Outdoor Education Centre.

Pass the village garage on the left and, opposite the single-storey former village bakery, now an antique shop, also on the left, cross Main Street and walk through the children's playground to the former row of railway workers' cottages. Walk along the path which now covers where the railway line originally ran.

Completed in 1882, the line consisted of a single track and the remains of the iron turntable required to swing the steam engines round for their return journey to Glasgow can be seen on the edge of the trees which line the path.

Follow the path 200 yards to where the site of the former railway station is now occupied by a large car park. Walk to the far side of the car park to visit the Scottish Wool Centre.

Notice the centre's unusual rooftop weathervane in the form of a horned ram and its window displays showing the process of sheep shearing. Enter to learn more about wool from the time it leaves the sheep's back until it reaches the backs of the fashion models in the shape of stylish garments.

On leaving the centre, with its range of shops, café and theatre where sheep and sheepdog shows are staged, look ahead to enjoy the view of Craigmore.

Translated from the Gaelic Craigmore means the Big Hill, and it dominates Aberfoyle. Craigmore was formerly quarried for its whinstone, used for local road construction.

Cross the car park to return to the tourist centre where this walk began.

Limecraig walk

Start at the car park at Aberfoyle Medical Centre at the eastern entrance to the village and walk up the narrow Forestry Commission road past the white-washed cottage on the right. After approximately quarter of a mile, at the top of the hill pass the former Aberfoyle Sawmill on the right and enter the grounds of Dounans Outdoor Education Centre. Walk past the playing field on the right on whose far side is the open-air amphitheatre and barbecue site constructed by the Royal Corps of Engineers in the mid-1980s.

The camp's wooden buildings were erected in 1940 and used first by Second World War evacuees from Glasgow.

Keeping strictly to the forest path, continue past the Assembly Hall, at whose entrance a plaque notes that after peace was declared in 1945 the camp was used to house refugees from the Netherlands. Pass the single-storey wooden block containing the camp manager's cottage and headmaster's house on the right and continue up the steep incline past the camp sickbay on the slope to the left. Notice the remains of the Second World War air-raid shelters. At the top of the slope cross the car park.

This may once have been the site of a small castle. Notice the large glacial boulders unearthed during excavations for the canoe pond in the mid-1980s.

Continue past the canoe pond on the left to where the path leaves the camp grounds. Walk on up the hill.

At the T-junction stop to look up at the wooded slopes of 1,000ft-high Limecraig. Limecraig takes its name from the lime kilns which were formerly operated on its slopes from the 1720s up to Victorian times, supplied with lime-stone quarried higher on its slopes and brought down by an incline tramway.

The lime was used both in agriculture by farmers to improve the quality of the soil in their fields and in Scottish industries such as the famous Carron Iron Works near Falkirk.

Turn left and follow the signed forest path through the wide variety of trees to the 55ft-high Waterfall of the Little Fawn.

The stream flowing from the foot of the falls is the Alt Vingen, which translated from the Gaelic means the Twiggy Torrent.

Retrace your steps to rejoin the forest path leading to the Highland Boundary Fault Trail and climb the steep hill to the Forest Centre.

Built in 1962 of locally quarried slate with a grant from the Carnegie (United Kingdom) Trust, the lodge houses information displays about the Queen Elizabeth Forest Park which is the largest in the UK. There is also a café, shop and toilet facilities. From the viewpoint look west to 1,271ft-high Craigmore, whose name means the Big Hill, and further on to the Duchray Hills and 3,192ft-high Ben Lomond.

From the main entrance to the Forest Centre walk down the hill past the Warden's Cottage on the left which is also built of Aberfoyle slate. Turn right and go down to the shores of the lochans. Walk on to the car park and turn left onto the Duke's Pass, built by the Duke of Montrose to enable his horse-drawn coaches to reach his hunting lodge overlooking Loch Achray. Descend the hill and look to the south to see the Covenanters Inn on the far hillside. Walk past the typically Scottish stone-built detached and semi-detached villas on the left and at the corner pass Aberfoyle Community Hall on the right. Continue on downhill.

Note the old stables on the right which formerly housed the horses used to pull wagonettes laden with visitors on outings to what in Victorian times was often described as Scotland's Lakeland. Following the Second World War the stables were used to accommodate the ponies used to introduce the sport of pony trekking to Scotland.

At the foot of the hill on the right pass the former premises of the public bar of the Bailie Nicol Jarvie Hotel, now converted into residential apartments.

On the left, at the junction with Main Street, notice the solid red sandstone-built premises of the Bank of Scotland. Before being converted into a bank office, this building was the home of the manager of the Aberfoyle Slate Quarries.

Turn left into Main Street and walk the length of it back to the car park at Aberfoyle Medical Centre where this trail began.

Inchmahome Island walk

At Port of Menteith board the ferry operated by Historic Scotland and sail across the waters of the Lake of Menteith to the island of Inchmahome.

During the short voyage notice on the shore the Gothic-style Menteith parish church, built in 1878, with its impressive tall spire, the stone-built mausoleum burial place of the Grahams of Gartmore and the attractive whitewashed premises of the Lake of Menteith Hotel. Note also the Lake of Menteith Fisheries Ltd's modern lodge and trout fishery.

After landing at the pier on Inchmahome, turn left and enter the ruins of the priory church by the west door.

The priory belonged to the Augustinian order of monks. The buildings date from 1238 when the priory was endowed by local laird Walter Comyn, fourth Earl of Menteith. Look to the left to see the remains of the former bell tower.

Walk on down the length of the pillared nave, noticing where the side altars were situated. Walk forward into the chancel.

After the Reformation took place in Scotland in 1560, when Protestant worship replaced that of the Roman Catholic Church, this part of the building was used as a burial place. The skull and crossbones carved on several of the stones is a symbol for death. In particular notice the flat gravestones which mark the burial places of the famous Don Roberto, MP and great adventurer, and his wife Gabrielle. Look at the symbols on the tombstones. On Don Roberto's stone pick out the brand mark which he used on his cattle when he was a gaucho, or cowboy, in South America. On Gabrielle's stone is one of the first depictions of the open-topped thistle, which later became the symbol of the Scottish National Party of which both Don Roberto and his wife were amongst the earliest supporters. Straight ahead notice the impressive remains of the window at the east end of the apse through which the first rays of the morning sun used to illuminate the high altar at the first service of worship early each morning. On the right are the sedilia, the stone seats on which the monks were permitted to rest during the lengthy service, and the piscina, the sink without a drain in which the gold and silver communion vessels were cleansed at the end of Mass so that the dregs of the wine were not washed away but allowed to seep slowly into the surrounding sandstone. Note also the aumbry, the small wall cupboard in which the communion vessels were stored.

Leave the church through the door on the right, as the monks would have done at the conclusion of worship, and enter the cloisters, the arched covered walk which provided them with shelter from the weather while they prayed or meditated. Turn left into the chapter house where the monks met after the first service of the day.

Here in the chapter house the prior read either a chapter from the Bible or from the book of rules of the order and it was from this that this important room took its name. Look at the carved figures of a knight and a monk, whose tonsure haircut is clearly visible. Most interesting are the stone figures of Walter Stewart, Earl of Menteith, and his countess wife, who are depicted with their dogs lying obediently at their feet. Notice also the large stone carved with the never-ending Celtic eternity chain.

Return to the cloisters and then on the left enter the small, narrow parlour, which took its name from the French verb *parler*, meaning to talk, which is what the monks were permitted to do here. Walk on to the warming room.

This was the only place in the priory where the monks enjoyed the luxury of a fire. On the outer wall on the left is the sink where the monks washed their hands before sitting down to eat their meals. Notice the remains of the stairway which led to the dormitory on the floor above where the monks slept. Continuing round the line of the foundations on the left is the site of the frater, a refectory or dining room, and on the far wall note the situation of the pulpit from which one of the brothers said grace at the start of each meal and read from the Bible as his fellow monks ate.

Walk round the remainder of the cloisters, noticing the lawn in the centre which was known as the Garth and where the monks are believed to have relaxed by playing a form of boules. Leave the cloisters and walk on to beyond the warming room to find the reredorter, the monks' lavatories.

These are one of the earliest examples of plumbing in Scotland, as they were designed to be flushed by water from the loch when the water level was sufficiently high.

Walk on to the banks of the island. Turn right and follow the path which skirts its shores, where there are large water lilies to be seen during the summer months.

The path also leads to the bower of trees where tradition claims that in 1547 the monks encouraged four-year-old Mary Queen of Scots and her young ladies-in-waiting to plant boxwood trees, to keep them occupied during the weeks which they spent on Inchmahome before being taken to Dumbarton on the Clyde to sail to France to seek safety at the royal court.

Toilets and a small visitor centre and shop are sited on the return route to the pier and the ferry back to the mainland. After disembarking from the ferry, the church, graveyard and Lake of Menteith Hotel and its grounds are all also worth visiting.

Index

If you are interested in purchasing other books published by Tempus,
or in case you have difficulty finding any Tempus books in your local bookshop,
you can also place orders directly through our website

www.tempus-publishing.com

or from

BOOKPOST, Freepost, PO Box 29, Douglas, Isle of Man IM99 1BQ
Tel 01624 836000   email bookshop@enterprise.net